Doing Business with the United Arab Emirates

GLOBAL MARKET BRIEFINGS

Doing Business with the United Arab Emirates

Second Edition

Consultant Editor:
Marat Terterov

Series editor:
Anthony Shoult

Published in association with:

Abu Dhabi Chamber of Commerce & Industry
www.abudhabichamber.ae

and

Dubai Chamber of Commerce & Industry
www.dcci.ae

GMB

Publisher's note

Every possible effort has been made to ensure that the information contained in this book is accurate at the time of going to press, and the publishers and authors cannot accept responsibility for any errors or omissions, however caused. No responsibility for loss or damage occasioned to any person acting, or refraining from action, as a result of the material in this publication can be accepted by the editor, the publisher or any of the authors.

This second edition first published in Great Britain and the United States in 2006 by GMB Publishing Limited

120 Pentonville Road
London N1 9JN
UK
www.globalmarketbriefings.com

22883 Quicksilver Drive
Sterling VA 20166-2012
USA

ISBN 1-905050-05-4

British Library Cataloguing-in-Publication Data

A CIP record for this book is available from the British Library

---

Library of Congress Cataloguing-in Publication Data

Typeset by Digital Publishing Solution
Printed and bound in Great Britain

Contents

Foreword

The economy of the UAE has performed admirably over the past few years and is poised to forge ahead with drive and confidence. Oil, considered by some as a curse, is an asset that the UAE has effectively used in order to diversify its economy and to establish its position in the international economic arena. The rise in oil income has afforded the UAE's economy an opportunity to mount a major drive on several fronts to create balanced growth across all economic sectors.

There is no secret formula for success. The prognosis is quite simple and direct. Our economic, legal and financial environment is business friendly, our policies are liberal and our infrastructure is complete and being developed to match the growing needs of our superstructure. And last but not least, our economic paradigm is based on the principles of *laissez-passer* and *laissez-faire*.

The UAE's people and government have inherited the legacy of the founding father of our modern country, the late President Sheikh Zayed Bin Sultan Al Nahyan, which is firmly founded on compassion, openness and unity. Our current president is intent on maintaining that legacy and building on it for a more prosperous economy and sustainable growth.

All the UAE's ministries are working very hard to create the legal structures needed to support the rapid growth within the UAE and meet the needs of the country's fast-increasing relationships with economies overseas. The government has already set the stage for expanded contractual, free-trade agreements with Europe, the USA, Australia, other non-Gulf countries, Arab countries, Latin America, our big neighbours in South and East Asia, our Red Sea neighbours in Africa and with the central Asian region. Yet, our priority is to cement our relations with the other Gulf Cooperation Council (GCC) members. Once we become a fully integrated economic region, our global economic position will be greatly enhanced.

We are also spearheading an aggressive privatization campaign that will open the door for local, regional and international business to become our partners. Our efforts to empower the private sector and decrease its dependence on government contracts and projects have already borne fruit and our private sector is proud of the entrepreneurial capabilities it demonstrated before and is revealing now.

I am truly confident that *Doing Business with the United Arab Emirates*, as a part of the acclaimed Global Market Briefings series, will provide comprehensive and accurate information, which honestly reflects our industrious economic reality. We believe that information is power, and the symmetry of information is an integral ingredient of sound business decision making. Information is also a prerequisite for good governance in both public and private-sector organizations.

The contributors to this valuable publication have done a monumental job, despite the complexity of the task. The book's sponsors should be applauded for their understanding of the need to promote their country to the elite of world business.

Shaikha Lubna Al Qasimi
Minister of Economy and Planning

Foreword

It gives me great pleasure to have been given this opportunity to welcome this new edition of *Doing Business with the United Arab Emirates*. I must thank all those involved in putting together such a detailed and comprehensive guide for the business community abroad.

The UAE is experiencing a boom, with growth estimated by the Central Bank to be not less than 10 per cent this year and much the same in 2006, due in part to high oil prices. But the growth is not only based on oil; the non-oil sector is flourishing and growth here is set to rise by nine per cent in 2006. Manufacturing and heavy industrial projects are rising fast and already contribute about 10 per cent of GDP. Tourism and related industries are booming too, with a contribution of 21 per cent to GDP. As anyone who has visited the Federation recently will know, real estate is now a huge business and is enjoying an unprecedented success.

The health of the economy was shown in the results of listed companies in 2004, which detailed profits of between 25 and 40 per cent being the norm. Some banks even doubled their net earnings over the previous year. And this trend continued into 2005.

It is against this backdrop of a thriving economy that we welcome foreign companies and foreign investment. The Federation is uniquely established as a hub for the whole region, where companies from all over the world are coming to set up their operations base, enjoying valuable tax and other benefits in the process.

Doing Business with the United Arab Emirates is an excellent compilation of considered and authoritative material from a variety of specialists, each with a detailed knowledge and understanding of the subject under review. I wish the book every success.

His Excellency Easa Saleh Al-Gurg CBE
United Arab Emirates Ambassador to the United Kingdom

About the Contributors

Dubai Chamber of Commerce and Industry (DCCI) began with 450 members and its management was assigned to a 12-member board of directors. It now offers value-added services such as data management and business research, mediation, arbitration, trade mission and delegation and entrepreneurial training in addition to commercial, foreign relations and business policy services. It also boasts a state-of-the art library and hosts trade fairs, conventions and exhibitions.

The many initiatives of DCCI that are contributing towards the progress of the business community include Dubai International Arbitration Centre, Dubai Ethics Resource Centre, Dubai University, Dubai Trade Point, Credit Rating Services and Dubai The City That Cares, an annual campaign directed towards boosting the retail and trade sector and aiding the local and international charity organizations.

The DCCI has notched up an exceptional string of achievements in the four decades since its foundation. Its members and officials, with the strong and unflinching support of the authorities in Dubai, have helped the organization achieve excellence in all its ventures. It continues its onward journey into a future that looks more promising than ever before.

EACM is a wholly owned subsidiary of Mellon Financial Corporation, one of the world's largest financial services companies. Mellon's mission is to deliver best-in-class investment products and services, providing clients with access to a broad range of specialist skills and expertise from a single platform. Mellon's unique model leverages the investment management capabilities of a diverse pool of specialist asset management companies, each of which is a separate entrepreneurial unit, free to pursue superior performance with its own distinctive investment process. This model creates an environment in which each asset manager can perform best. This exclusive group of specialist companies today manages a comprehensive range of investment strategies with combined assets under management of US$766.1 billion (source: Mellon, September 2005). Mellon has a branch office in Dubai, which is regulated by the Dubai Financial Services Authority.

Paul Holmes has an honours degree in Economics and is an Associate of the Chartered Insurance Institute. He has more than 20 years' experience in the industry, working in a variety of managerial positions in the UK and overseas. Over the last 10 years, he has managed different Middle Eastern territories for Norwich Union and, more recently, AXA following the Middle East merger of the two operations.

InCite is a full-service market research agency with operations throughout the Arabian Peninsula. Established in 1994 the company has offices in Bahrain, Qatar, Kuwait, Saudi Arabia and the UAE. With quantitative and qualitative research expertise, InCite conducts studies among consumers as well as at the business-to-business and industrial level.

Jan Stuffers is Managing Consultant at InCite Research & Marketing Solutions.

KPMG is one of the world's largest professional services firms, operating in over 825 cities in 157 countries, and is the global leader in providing services to businesses around the world. KPMG's strength is its international network, made up of strong national practices combined with its emphasis on proving market-specific added service to meet its clients' needs in a rapidly changing business environment.

Trowers & Hamlins is a long-established international law firm with 80 partners and over 500 staff. It provides the full range of corporate, business and commercial legal services and has a substantial client base in both the private and public sectors. Its principal office is located in the City of London, while overseas offices are located in Abu Dhabi, Bahrain, Dubai, Egypt and Oman. Trowers & Hamlins also has an association with the leading Saudi Arabian law firm of Hassan Mahassni.

An award-winning firm, Trowers & Hamlins' prominence derives from a long-term commitment to the Middle East. With some 60 lawyers, including 14 partners, living and working in the Middle East, it provides a full client service to regional governmental institutions and to a large number of multinationals and other organizations. Trowers & Hamlins is known principally for its project and company/commercial work and has advised on a number of the largest, most prestigious and innovative projects in the region. These have been in the utilities, infrastructure, industrial and hydrocarbon sectors among others.

Empowering Business Through
Wireless Solutions.....

MENA Region

Emitac Mobile Solutions, LLC.
P.O. Box 8391
Dubai, United Arab Emirates
Phone: +971-4-349-0955
Fax: +971-4-283-0861
Web: http://emsmobile.com

Doing Business in the UAE

Emitac Mobile Solutions, LLC. (EMS) is a Dubai based solutions and service provider focused on the delivery, implementation, and support of BlackBerry® Solutions in the Middle East, North Africa and the Eastern European Region. Since 1998 the company's management team has been involved in the delivery of BlackBerry and other handheld mobile solutions throughout the United States, Europe and Asia and in 2006, became a Research In Motion® (RIM) certified BlackBerry Strategic Channel Partner for the region. EMS is the region's first Mobile Virtual Solutions Provider (MVSP). EMS provides a variety of mobile services for the mobile operator and enterprise customer, delivered by an experienced team of mobile professionals, that includes BlackBerry go-to-market services, sales, marketing, distribution, technical support, mobile application design, development, implementation and technical support. BlackBerry is a wireless communications solution designed for mobile professionals and enterprises who want to quickly and easily manage their business and personal communications while on the move. BlackBerry is developed and manufactured by RIM and there are currently over five million BlackBerry subscribers worldwide. BlackBerry is number one in the global PDA space, with 21% of the market share.

BlackBerry is an end-to-end wireless solution that, combined with a network operator's wireless data network, comprises advanced, lightweight devices, software and services to provide users with a wireless extension of all their communications needs. Wireless services include email, voice, SMS and browsing. For enterprise users, these extend to calendar, Internet and intranet browsing plus the ability to access other corporate data stored behind the company firewall. In addition the BlackBerry device supports wireless access to a user's personal organiser information.

With its "always on, always connected" functionality, the BlackBerry device remains connected at all times. Email is pushed directly to the device when it arrives at the inbox. The BlackBerry Solution is a superior and preferred concept for mobilizing and making enterprise email and corporate data applications pervasive. The BlackBerry Platform advantages include:

- Approved global security model, 3DES and/or ADES encryption
- Supports secure access to corporate data, applications and web services.
- Centralized service and device management
- Over The Air (OTA provisioning)
- Deployed by government, public safety and Fortune 1000 organizations worldwide

- Solutions available for the extension of enterprise applications (SAP, Oracle, Siebel, Remedy, etc.)

Users are able to simplify communications and streamline their lifestyle to accomplish more and focus on what's important, managing and growing their business.

For the Enterprise: *Empowering Business through Wireless Solutions!*

Working with the local mobile operator, EMS provides end-to-end support for implementing the BlackBerry Solution as well as other mobile applications for the enterprise business customer.

To add to the overall effectiveness of the BlackBerry experience, EMS works with local information providers to develop "localized" content solutions targeted for the marketplace. EMS believes that this content provides a unique offering that will increase customer acquisition and improve subscriber retention while protecting the mobile operator from competitive offerings.

Utilizing unique and proprietary leading edge mobile development tools, EMS provides corporate customers with the ability to extend their enterprise applications to the BlackBerry supported handhelds. This combination of product delivery and customised wireless enterprise applications provides enterprises with a significant competitive edge and differentiator while providing mobile professionals with the necessary tools to stay connected and up to date.

To fulfil this effort, EMS provides a unique wireless application platform, mobile studio and web based services to easily create and deploy secure wireless handheld applications within a business enterprise;

- Horizontal applications to allow mobile users to access corporate data and documents from a wireless handheld device that are not otherwise available;
- Industry specific applications and branded content such as the latest financial market data to meet the needs of customers in Financial Services, Oil & Gas, Pharmaceutical and other markets;
- A proven methodology to manage the creation, deployment and management of wireless enterprise applications.

For the Mobile Operator: *Empowered to Deliver Enterprise Wireless Solutions!*

EMS offers unique services to Mobile Operators to ensure the successful end-to-end deployment of the BlackBerry Solution. Based on years of experience, EMS delivers robust go-to-market support that includes; development and implementation of the overall BlackBerry marketing plan and launch. Dedicated EMS resources work hand-in-hand with business, marketing, engineering, technology and customer support teams to complete the entire project and ensure the successful delivery of the BlackBerry Solution to the local market. Additionally, a dedicated Project Manager will be assigned who is the central point for the development of an overall implementation plan, and manages all communications, project tasks and deliverables throughout the project.

Project Development and Deployment Services:

- EMS, alongside the Mobile Operator, will develop an all encompassing implementation plan which covers areas such as business planning, engineering, operations and customer support, business development, sales, and pre-launch and launch activities.
    - Business planning includes assisting in the development of the financial business model and executive presentation preparation.
    - Pre-launch activities include high profile, executive and government official user programs such as events to introduce the BlackBerry Solution; including media and social events.
    - At launch, both advertising and a public relations strategy are implemented to ensure as much exposure as possible for the Mobile Operator's offered BlackBerry Services. This includes the education to the market on the benefits of the solution as well as seminars and key note speakers at targeted events where appropriate.
- As each individual market is different, in addition to the above, tailored programs will be designed to address the specific needs of the market.
- Pre and post-sales support is provided by EMS on an ongoing basis and emphasizes a speed-to-market deployment that does not compromise the quality of experience already delivered by Mobile Operators that their customers are accustomed to.
- Business Development Services are offered to assist and advise in the definition and execution of sales strategies and processes to optimize the Mobile Operator' sales resources and drive sales quickly, effectively and efficiently.
- EMS will work side by side with the Mobile Operator's sales force to ensure successful customer presentations, closure of sales and product deployment. A local team of sales professionals with existing carrier and vertical market expertise, assisted by Technical Account

Managers and a team of Customer Support Representatives, supports the launch and ongoing BlackBerry sales efforts.

- Furthermore, EMS facilitates workshops with mobile operators and strategic customers who are deploying the BlackBerry Solution, to allow for further enhancement of strategies and processes based on customer feedback, while taking into account their specific requirements, locally, regionally and globally.

Technical and Customer Support and Logistics

A comprehensive technical support strategy, testing protocol and support plan based on years of EMS experience is implemented to support customers who subscribe to the Operator's BlackBerry offering.

- EMS dedicated call center support facilitates both Tier II and Tier III customer support and is integrated with the mobile operators existing Tier I customer care call center infrastructure to ensure effective customer management.
- The call center is staffed by RIM BlackBerry certified resources. EMS Customer Support provides the flexibility to operate on a 24 × 7 basis as appropriate for the Operator.
- Troubleshooting, incident reporting, and trouble ticket resolution is handled by the EMS call center.
- Dedicated resources are available to support the call center and will provide on site technicians to resolve customer issues when required.
- EMS manages all distribution activities from ordering to shipping, importing, and all other logistics of the BlackBerry handhelds and software directly to Mobile Operators, enterprise customers and retail outlets.
- Retail outlet personnel are trained by EMS staff to ensure an optimal customer experience when purchasing the BlackBerry handheld devices and services.

EMS offers a comprehensive approach to both mobile operators and enterprise customers to take advantage and the most up to date mobile technology available. For more information about EMS please visit the Company website at http://www.emsmobile.com

EMS NOW IN THE UAE
Empowering Business through Wireless Solutions
EMS
BlackBerry
log on today
www.emsmobile.com

Part One
Country Background

1.1

Historical, Geographic and Political Overview

Data Management and Business Research Department, DCCI

Geographical location and area

The United Arab Emirates (UAE) is a federal sovereign state that consists of seven emirates, namely: Abu Dhabi, Dubai, Sharjah, Ajman, Umm al-Quwain, Fujairah and Ras al-Khaimah. The federation was established on 2 December 1971, then the emirate of Ras al-Khaimah joined on 10 February 1972.

The UAE lies on the eastern coast of the Arabian Peninsula in the southwestern corner of the Arabian Gulf. It is bounded to the northwest by the Arabian Gulf, to the east and southeast by the Sultanate of Oman and to the west and southwest by Saudi Arabia; part of its eastern boundary lies on the Gulf of Oman. The total area of the UAE is approximately 77,700 sq km, excluding the small dependent islands.

Population and language

In addition to its native population, the UAE is inhabited by a mixture of Arab nationals, Asians and Europeans. UAE society is distinguished by a high population growth rate due to rapid economic and social development. In 2003 the population of the UAE reached 4,041,000, as shown in Table 1.1.1.

The official language of the UAE is Arabic according to the constitution of the country, although English is also widely used, especially in the business and trade sectors. Expatriates use, unofficially, their mother tongues according to their nationalities.

Only 27 per cent of the total population of 4.041 million are UAE citizens. The rest include significant numbers of other Arabs – Palestinians, Egyptians, Jordanians, Yemenis, Omanis – as well as many Iranians, Pakistanis, Indians, Filipinos, and west Europeans. The majority of UAE citizens are Sunni Muslims with a small Shi'a minority. Most foreigners also are Muslim, although Hindus and Christians make up a portion of the UAE's foreign population.

Table 1.1.1 Total UAE population 1975–2003

	Year				
Emirate	**2003***	**1995†**	**1985†**	**1980†**	**1975†**
Abu Dhabi	1,591,000	942,463	566,036	451,848	211,812
Dubai	1,204,000	689,420	370,788	276,301	183,187
Sharjah	636,000	402,792	228,317	159,317	78,790
Ajman	235,000	121,491	54,546	36,100	16,690
Umm al-Quwain	62,000	35,361	19,285	12,426	6,908
Ras al-Khaimah	195,000	143,334	96,578	73,918	43,845
Fujairah	118,000	76,180	43,753	32,189	16,655
Total	4,041,000	2,411,041	1,379,303	1,042,099	557,887

*estimated †census data (Dec)

Source: Ministry of Planning 2004

Educational standards among the UAE population are rising rapidly; citizens and temporary residents have taken advantage of facilities throughout the country. The UAE University in Al Ain had roughly 16,000 students in 2000 and a network of technical/vocational colleges opened in 1989. The government expenditure on education stood at AED5.38 billion in 2003.

Climate

The UAE lies in an arid, tropical zone. Its climate is characterized by high temperatures and humidity in summer and a moderate winter accompanied by irregular rainfalls, the annual average of which rarely exceeds between 5 and 10 inches.

The average temperature throughout the year is around 75°F (24°C) as shown in Table 1.1.2. The summer season extends from May to October, during which the temperature varies from 113–122°F

(30–47°C). The northern wind in summer reduces the temperature while, in winter, it declines to an average that varies from 60–70°F (12–26°C).

Table 1.1.2. Average temperature and humidity in Dubai during 2001

Month	Average temperature (°C)		Average humidity (%)	
	Minimum	Maximum	Minimum	Maximum
January	14.0	23.9	45	83
February	15.1	25.0	42	83
March	17.2	27.7	39	82
April	20.4	32.5	32	77
May	24.0	37.2	27	73
June	26.6	39.2	30	79
July	29.4	40.7	32	77
August	29.9	41.1	31	75
September	27.0	38.8	31	81
October	23.4	35.2	34	81
November	19.5	30.6	39	80
December	15.8	26.2	45	83

Source: Dubai Civil Aviation Dept, Meteorological Section

History

The UAE was formed from the group of tribally organized Arabian Peninsula sheikhdoms along the southern coast of the Persian Gulf and the northwestern coast of the Gulf of Oman. This area was converted to Islam in the 7th century; for centuries it was embroiled in dynastic disputes. It became known as the Pirate Coast as raiders based there harassed foreign shipping, although both European and Arab navies patrolled the area from the 17th century into the 19th century.

Early British expeditions to protect the Indian trade from raiders at Ras al- Khaimah led to campaigns against that headquarters and other harbours along the coast in 1819. The next year, a general peace treaty was signed to which all the principal sheikhs of the coast adhered. Raids continued intermittently until 1835, when the sheikhs agreed not to engage in hostilities at sea. In 1853, they signed a treaty with the UK, under which the sheikhs (the 'Trucial Sheikhdoms') agreed to a 'perpetual maritime truce'. It was enforced by the UK, and disputes among sheikhs were referred to the British for settlement.

Primarily in reaction to the ambitions of other European countries, the UK and the Trucial Sheikhdoms established closer bonds in an 1892 treaty, similar to treaties entered into by the UK with other Gulf principalities. The sheikhs agreed not to dispose of any territory except to the UK and not to enter into relationships with any foreign government other than the UK without its consent. In return, the British promised to protect the Trucial Coast from all aggression by sea and to help out in case of land attack.

In 1955, the UK sided with Abu Dhabi in the latter's dispute with Saudi Arabia over the Buraimi Oasis and other territories to the south. A 1974 agreement between Abu Dhabi and Saudi Arabia would have settled the Abu Dhabi–Saudi border dispute, however the agreement has yet to be ratified by the UAE government and is not recognized by the Saudi government. The border with Oman also remains officially unsettled, but the two governments agreed to delineate the border in May 1999.

In 1968, the UK announced its decision, reaffirmed in March 1971, to end the treaty relationships with the seven Trucial Sheikhdoms that had been, together with Bahrain and Qatar, under British protection. The nine attempted to form a union of Arab emirates, but by mid-1971 they were unable to agree on terms of union, even though the termination date of the British treaty relationship was the end of 1971. Bahrain became independent in August 1971 and Qatar in September of the same year. When the British–Trucial Sheikhdoms treaty expired on 1 December 1971 all seven became fully independent. On 2 December 1971 six of them entered into a union called the United Arab Emirates. The seventh, Ras al-Khaimah, joined in early 1972.

Political system

According to the constitution, the Supreme Council of the federation is the highest political authority in the country. It consists of all the rulers of the seven emirates. The president and the vice-president of the state are elected by the Supreme Council and from its members. The president appoints the prime minister with the consent of the members of the Supreme Council. The members of the federal government are appointed by a decree by the president upon the recommendation of the prime minister. The constitution established the positions of president (chief of state) and vice president, each serving five-year terms; a Council of Ministers (cabinet), led by a prime minister (head of government); a Supreme Council of rulers; and a

40-member Federal National Council (FNC) – a consultative body whose members are appointed by the emirate rulers.

The FNC, which consists of representatives of each emirate, is the legislative council (parliament). It exercises the authority to discuss and sanction all federal laws and then refer them to the Supreme Council for enactment. This is in addition to its role of discussing the issues of interest to the citizen and controlling the performance of the federal government.

Administratively, the UAE is a loose federation of seven emirates, each with its own ruler. The pace at which local government in each emirate evolves from traditional to modern is set primarily by the ruler. Under the provisional constitution of 1971, each emirate reserves considerable powers, including control over mineral rights (notably oil) and revenues. In this milieu, federal powers have developed slowly. The relative political and financial influence of each emirate is reflected in the allocation of positions in the federal government. The ruler of Abu Dhabi, whose emirate is the UAE's major oil producer, is president of the UAE. The ruler of Dubai, which is the UAE's commercial centre and a significant oil producer, is vice president and prime minister.

Since achieving independence in 1971, the UAE has worked to strengthen its federal institutions. Nonetheless, each emirate still retains substantial autonomy and progress toward greater federal integration has slowed in recent years. A basic concept in the UAE government's development as a federal system is that a significant percentage of each emirate's revenues should be devoted to the UAE central budget.

The UAE has no political parties. There is talk of steps toward democratic government, but nothing concrete has emerged. The rulers hold power on the basis of their dynastic position and their legitimacy in a system of tribal consensus. Rapid modernization, enormous strides in education and the influx of a large foreign population have changed the face of the society but have not fundamentally altered this traditional political system.

Defence

The Trucial Oman Scouts, long the symbol of public order on the coast and commanded by British officers, were turned over to the UAE as its defence forces in 1971. The UAE armed forces, consisting of 65,000 troops, are headquartered in Abu Dhabi and are primarily responsible for the defence of the seven emirates.

The UAE military relies heavily on troop force from other Arab countries and Pakistan. The officer corps, however, is composed almost exclusively of UAE nationals.

The UAE air force has about 3,500 personnel. The air force agreed in 1999 to purchase 80 advanced US F-16 multirole fighter aircraft. Other equipment includes French Mirage 3s and 5s and Mirage 2000s, British Hawk aircraft, and French helicopters. The air defence has a Hawk missile programme for which the USA is providing training. The UAE has taken delivery of two of five Triad I-Hawk batteries. The UAE's navy is small – about 1,500 personnel – and maintains 12 well-equipped coastal patrol boats and eight missile crafts.

The UAE sent forces to liberate Kuwait during the 1990–91 Gulf War. In addition, it continues to contribute to the continued security and stability of the Gulf and the Straits of Hormuz. It is a leading partner in the campaign against terrorism, providing assistance in the military, diplomatic and financial arenas. The UAE military provides humanitarian assistance to Iraq.

Foreign relations

The UAE joined the United Nations (UN) and the Arab League and has established diplomatic relations with more than 60 countries, including the USA, Japan, Russia, the People's Republic of China and most western European countries. It has played a moderate role in the Organization of Petroleum Exporting Countries (OPEC), the Organization of Arab Petroleum Exporting Countries, the UN and the Gulf Cooperation Council (GCC).

Substantial development assistance has increased the UAE's stature among recipient states. Most of this foreign aid (in excess of US$15 billion) has been to Arab and Muslim countries. Following Iraq's 1990 invasion and attempted annexation of Kuwait, the UAE has sought to rely on the GCC, the USA and other Western allies for its security. The UAE believes that the Arab League needs to be restructured to become a viable institution and would like to increase strength and interoperability of the GCC defence forces.

On the international level the UAE is a member of, among others:

- the Arab League;
- the GCC;
- the UN;
- the World Bank for Reconstruction and Development;

- the International Monetary Fund (IMF);
- the International Labour Organization;
- the United Nations Educational, Scientific and Cultural Organization (UNESCO);
- the Organization of the Islamic Conference;
- the International Organization for Industrial Development;
- the World Health Organization (WHO).

Being an important oil-producing country, it is also a member of OPEC and the Organization of Arab Petroleum Exporting Countries (OAPEC).

UAE: facts in brief

Official name

United Arab Emirates

Geography

Area: 82,880 sq km (30,000 sq miles) – roughly the size of Maine, USA.
Cities: Abu Dhabi (capital, pop. 1,000,000); Dubai (pop. 860,000). These population figures are based on 2002 estimates.
Terrain: Largely desert with some agricultural areas.
Climate: Hot, humid, low annual rainfall.

People

Nationality: UAE, Emirati (noun and adjective).
Population: 4.041 million, of which 808,200 (20 per cent) are locals and 3.32 million (80 per cent) expatriates.
Annual growth rate: 7.6 per cent.
Ethnic groups: Arab, Pakistani, Indian, Iranian, Filipino (27 per cent of residents are UAE citizens).
Religions: Muslim (96 per cent), Hindu, Christian.
Languages: Arabic (official), English, Hindi, Urdu, Persian.
Education: The United Nation's Development Programme (UNDP) Human Development Index (HDI) ranking is 49. Estimated net primary school enrolment rate (2001–02) is 81 per cent.

Adult literacy rate (percentage aged 15 years and over HDI (2002)) is 77.3 per cent for the overall population. Adult literacy rate (percentage aged 15 years and above) for males is 75.6 per cent and 80.7 per cent for females.
Health: Infant mortality rate (2002) is 8 per 1,000 live births. Life expectancy at birth (2000–05) is 74 years with male life expectancy at birth at 73.2 years (2002) and that for females at 77.3 years (2002). The crude death rate is 2 per 1,000 of the population (Unicef, 2003). The under-five-year mortality rate (2002) is 8 per 1,000 live births. There are 313.2 internet users (2002) per 1,000 people.

Government

Type: Federation of emirates.
Independence: 2 December 1971.
Provisional constitution: 2 December 1971.
Branches: Executive – 7-member Supreme Council of Rulers, which elects president and vice president; legislative – 40-member FNC (consultative only); judicial – Islamic and secular courts.
Administrative subdivisions: seven largely self-governing city-states.
Political parties: None.
Suffrage: None.
Central government budget (2002): US$6.3 billion.

Economy

Currency: Dirham (AED).
Foreign direct investment (FDI) inflows (2003): US$480 million.
GDP (2003): US$79.81 billion. In 2003, GDP growth rate was 12.5 per cent and per capita GDP was US$19,751.
GDP breakdown by sector (2003): Oil and gas (31.9 per cent), agriculture (3.1 per cent), manufacturing (13.6 per cent), construction (6.4 per cent), finance and insurance (6.2 per cent) and real estate (7.2 per cent).
Government budget (2003): –4.6 per cent of GDP, US$3.7 billion deficit.
Trade balance: 25.2 per cent of GDP.
Exports: US$65.8 billion, of which oil and gas constituted 44.9 per cent of total exports. Other exports included chemicals, base metals, textiles and foodstuffs. Major markets for non-oil

exports included Japan (20 per cent), UK (6.4 per cent), China (6.1 per cent), Germany (3.5 per cent) and India (2.8 per cent).
Imports: US$45.7 billion, including food, construction materials, vehicles and parts and clothing. Major suppliers included Japan (10.7 per cent), USA (9.3 per cent), China (8 per cent), Germany (7.7 per cent), UK (7.4 per cent) and India (6.8 per cent).
Transparency International's Corruption Perception Index: score of 6.1, rated 29th internationally.

1.2

Economic Overview and Outlook for 2005–06

ADCCI

Introduction

Prior to the first exports of oil in 1962, the UAE's economy was dominated by pearl production, fishing, agriculture and herding. Since the rise of oil prices in 1973, however, petroleum has dominated the economy, accounting for most of its export earnings and providing significant opportunities for investment. The UAE has huge proven oil reserves – estimated at 98.2 billion barrels in 1998 – with gas reserves estimated at 5.8 billion cubic metres; at present production rates, these supplies would last well over 150 years.

In 2003, the UAE produced some 2.3 million barrels of oil per day. Of this, Abu Dhabi produced approximately 85 per cent; Dubai and Sharjah, to a much lesser extent, produced the rest.

Major increases in imports occurred in manufactured goods, machinery and transportation equipment, which together accounted for 70 per cent of total imports. Another important foreign exchange earner, the Abu Dhabi Investment Authority (which controls the investments of Abu Dhabi, the wealthiest emirate) manages an estimated US$150 billion in overseas investments.

More than 200 factories operate at the Jebel Ali complex in Dubai, which includes a deep-water port and a free-trade zone for manufacturing and distribution in which all goods for re-export or transshipment enjoy a 100 per cent duty exemption. A major power plant with associated water desalination units, an aluminum smelter and a steel fabrication unit are prominent facilities in the complex.

Except in the free-trade zone, the UAE requires at least 51 per cent local citizen ownership in all businesses operating in the country as part of its attempt to place Emiratis into leadership positions.

As a member of the Gulf Cooperation Council (GCC), the UAE participates in the wide range of GCC activities that focus on economic issues. These include regular consultations and development of common policies covering trade, investment, banking and finance, transportation, telecommunications and other technical areas, including protection of intellectual property rights.

Economic policy making in the UAE

The UAE's economy has witnessed rapid stages of development. Even before 1957, the economy of those emirates constituting the federation, under their self-ruling system, was dependent on the natural and human resources available. Economic resources varied in each emirate in accordance with the area, population and the abundance of the resources of each of them. The economy concentrated on activities such as pearl diving, fishing, trade, agriculture, grazing and some handicraft industries. Each emirate was distinguished by its relative dependence on a special economic source according to its nature and the availability of human skills.

In 1957, another stage of economic development started; it was the beginning of the era of oil producing and exporting in Abu Dhabi. Dubai followed suit in 1969, and then Sharjah did the same. This stage has witnessed the increasing importance of the oil sector because of the huge amount of revenues it provided in comparison with other sources of the national income that led to the decrease of the importance of the traditional economic activities, the first of which was the sector of pearl diving and trading. Since then, oil and its related industries have become the backbone of the UAE's economy.

At the end of 1971, a new stage had started with the constitution of the UAE, which necessitated the merger of the emirates' economies and utilizing available resources to build up the country and form a unified economic entity. The federal government tackled the different economic conditions in those emirates constituting the federation by working out economic plans on a federal level in order to build a modern society and a state. This included setting up an infrastructure and providing essential services, such as education, health services, road construction, supply of energy, establishing communication networks and others. Table 1.2.1 shows the UAE GDP at factor cost by economic sector from 1999 to 2003.

The economic resources in the UAE are generally characterized by the lack of natural resources except oil, natural gas and some raw materials. This made oil rank first among the other economic resources. The lack of human resources obliged the country to depend on expatriate labour, which led to the emergence of a demographic structure different from that which existed before 1957 and 1971.

Table 1.2.1. UAE GDP at factor cost by economic sector 1999 – 2003 (AED million)

Sector	Year				
	1999	2000	2001	2002	2003 *
Agriculture, livestock and fishing	7,551	9,047	8,862	9,105	9,359
Mining and quarrying	50,450	87,372	75,687	73,277	94,134
Manufacturing	26,539	34,762	35,132	36,673	40,100
Electricity, gas and water	4,416	4,615	4,890	5,274	5,513
Construction	16,621	16,857	17,446	17,988	18,791
Wholesale, retail and repairing services, restaurants and hotels	26,255	27,294	28,273	30,386	32,119
Transports, storage and communication	15,247	17,247	19,595	21,742	23,629
Financial corporation sector	13,663	14,862	16,845	17,314	18,394
Real estate and business services	18,384	19,068	19,662	20,388	21,205
Social and personal services	3,515	3,824	4,067	4,368	4,576
Less: imputed bank services	4,858	4,171	5,192	5,700	6,039
Government services	22,458	25,561	27,029	28,525	29,272
Domestic household services	1,556	1,641	1,940	2,030	2,068
Total GDP	201,797	257,979	254,236	261,370	293,121

*preliminary

Source: Ministry of Planning

The economic policy of the UAE is based on safeguarding and respecting the individual freedom in ownership of the means of production, practising any type of business activity and providing all facilities. There are no restrictions on imports and exports except some minor customs and administrative duties. The government also plays a supervisory role in issuing legislation that organizes the functioning of the various economic sectors while causing no hindrance to business activities. Simultaneously, these legislations protect the private rights and properties within the framework of the government's efforts to promote and elevate the community to an advanced standard of development and production.

Table 1.2.2 shows the main economic indicators of the UAE during the years 2000–03.

Table 1.2.2. Main economic indicators of UAE

Indicator (AED billion *)	2003 †	2002	2001	2000
GDP	293.1	261.4	254.2	258.0
Net national income	239.0	213.0	222.7	229.0
National savings	49.3	37.4	62.6	75.4
Final consumption expenditure	188.7	174.6	160.3	152.6
Final government cons	43.5	42.5	41.8	40.0
Final private cons	145.2	132.0	118.6	112.6
Gross fixed capital formation	63.0	61.0	60.2	57.4
Compensation of emp.	79.3	75.8	70.9	65.6
Per capita national income (AED)‡	59.2	56.7	63.8	70.5
US$	16.1	15.4	17.4	19.2
Per capita final consumption expenditure (AED)‡	46.7	46.5	46.0	47.0
US$	12.7	12.7	12.5	12.8
General average wage (AED)‡	33.9	33.4	33.2	34.2
US$	9.2	9.1	9.0	9.3
General average of labour Pord (AED)‡	88.5	90.0	93.0	96.8
US$	24.1	24.5	25.3	26.4

*unless specified otherwise †preliminary data ‡value in thousands

Source: Ministry of Planning

Mainstream economic policy outlook 2005–06

Sheikh Khalifa bin Zayed al-Nahyan will continue to cement his already strong position following his appointment as president of the UAE in November 2004, after the death of his father, Sheikh Zayed bin Sultan al-Nahyan. Sheikh Khalifa will maintain the relatively liberal social and economic policies of his father, ensuring support both from UAE nationals and expatriates and from among the ruling families of the UAE. The programme of economic reform and liberalization will continue and may pick up some pace, because of both the new ruler's leadership and the WTO.

Real GDP growth will pick up speed, bolstered by high oil earnings and sustained expansion in the non-oil economy. The fiscal deficit will remain very low by historical standards throughout the forecast period, despite significant gains in expenditure. The trade and current accounts will continue to generate large surpluses. There is no realistic prospect of the currency's peg to the US dollar coming under strain.

Fiscal policy outlook

With UAE oil production and global oil prices rising, we estimate that total fiscal earnings reached AED92.7 billion (US$25.2 billion) in 2004 – a year-on-year increase of 22 per cent and an all-time high. We expect that this will be exceeded in 2005, with upward adjustments to the forecast for oil prices pointing towards total revenue of around AED105 billion. Revenue will drop by around 6 per cent in 2006 as oil prices ease but, at AED99 billion, these will be stronger than in any year other than 2005.

Although it was previously assumed that expenditure would rise strongly over the forecast period, we have raised our projections following the government's recent decision to introduce very large public-sector pay increases. Together with other rises (particularly in capital expenditure), we believe that this will drive spending upwards by an annual average of around 10 per cent over the forecast period.

Overall, we forecast that this will result in a consolidated budget deficit of AED1.2 billion (0.3 per cent of GDP) in 2005, compared with an estimated shortfall of AED2.4 billion (0.7 per cent of GDP) in 2004. The deficit will widen to AED15.4 billion (4.5 per cent of GDP) in 2006. The outturn estimated for 2004 and that expected for 2005 should be the strongest recorded since the oil boom of 1970s, and even the deficit projected for 2006 will be well below the 10-year average.

Monetary policy outlook

Domestic interest rates will continue to track those in the USA closely. As US inflationary pressures persist, we expect US rates to continue to rise over the forecast period from the lows of recent years. This will see a steady return of local rates towards their historical averages. Despite evidence of mounting inflationary pressures within the economy, there has been no indication that the Central Bank of the UAE is preparing to increase the differential between local and US rates, which seems likely to remain narrow this year and next.

Inflation outlook

Inflation appears to have picked up as the booming economy has generated price pressures, particularly in the real estate sector and some parts of the service sectors. This has begun to drive up wage demands in the private sector – a trend that will be compounded by the large pay increases recently announced for government workers. The continued weakening of the US dollar (and, by extension, the dirham) against the currencies of the UAE's main trade partners will raise the average price of a range of imported goods, although the impact of this will be partly offset by the weakening of global commodity prices.

International indicators outlook

We estimate that global growth (measured using purchasing power parity exchange rates) reached 5.1 per cent in 2004, driven primarily by rapid expansion in the USA. We expect global growth to ease slightly but remain strong at 4.3 per cent and 4 per cent in 2005 and 2006 respectively, as slower US expansion is largely offset by a more marked pick-up in EU demand.

We continue to expect oil prices to remain very high as oil consumption continues to show growth, particularly in those Asian countries that do not belong to the Organization of Economic Cooperation and Development (OECD). Supply will struggle to keep pace, curbed by production problems in key exporting countries such as Iraq, Nigeria and Venezuela and a slowdown in growth in Russia. This will leave little spare capacity, which, with political tensions in the Gulf remaining significant, is likely to see the benchmark dated Brent Blend average around US$46/barrel this year – an increase of 20 per cent on last year's performance and an all-time high.

The market is expected to loosen in 2006 as production gains outstrip increases in demand, but prices will remain very high at US$40/barrel – more than US$10/barrel above the five-year average. In neither year of the forecast period do we expect the Organization of the Exporting Petroleum Companies (OPEC) to enforce production quotas, allowing UAE output to trend upward.

Economic growth outlook

The UAE economy is expected to grow at an average annual rate of around 6.5 per cent in real terms over the forecast period. Industrial growth will be the mainstay of the overall expansion, underpinned by continued, albeit modest, rises in oil production, as high prices allow OPEC to hold back from enforcing quota levels.

Table 1.2.3. International assumptions summary

	2003	2004	2005	2006
Real GDP growth				
World	3.9	5.1	4.2	3.9
OECD	2.0	3.3	2.4	2.3
EU25	1.1	2.4	1.9	2.1
		Exchange rates		
Yen: US dollar	115.9	108.1	102.7	93.8
US dollar: euro	1.132	1.244	1.350	1.400
SDR:US dollar	0.714	0.675	0.646	0.628
Financial indicators				
Yen 2-month private bill rate	0.03	0.00	0.05	0.34
US dollar 3-month commercial paper rate	1.10	1.48	3.31	4.38
Commodity prices				
Oil (Brent; US$/barrel)	28.8	38.5	46.0	40.0
Gold (US$/troy oz)	363.3	409.5	435.0	402.5
Food, feedstuffs and beverages (% change in US$ terms)	6.6	9.1	−6.5	−1.4
Industrial raw materials (% change in US$ terms)	13.0	21.0	3.5	−6.7

Note: Regional GDP growth rates weighted using purchasing power parity exchange rates.
Source: Economist Intelligence Unit (EIU)

Growth in non-oil industrial output will be a more important direct driver, however, as investment in manufacturing and heavier industrial projects (focused mainly on energy-intensive sectors such as petrochemicals and metals) brings new capacity on stream and the competitiveness of UAE exports is bolstered by the weakness of the US dollar.

Domestic and foreign investment in new projects is expected to remain strong, while capital spending on real estate and infrastructure schemes (including new roads and high-profile programmes, such as the proposed Dubai Light Railway) will also stay high. The service sector is also expected to attract substantial investment.

Recurrent demand for services is likely to pick up, led by the tourism industry, which has shown itself resilient to instability elsewhere in the region. Continued rapid growth in the population, fuelled largely by increases in the size of the expatriate workforce, will also underpin robust domestic demand, as will the recently announced public-sector pay increases, particularly as they are also likely to push private-sector pay settlements upwards.

Exchange rates outlook

There is little prospect of a change in the exchange-rate regime, and we expect the dirham to remain pegged to the US dollar at the current value of AED3.67:US$1 over the forecast period. Confidence in the peg remains high, bolstered by the Central Bank's long track record of maintaining the dollar value of the dirham and its absolute commitment to holding the peg in place. The forecast strength of the UAE's foreign-exchange earnings makes it highly unlikely that there will be any pressure on the peg, particularly as the Central Bank will be careful to ensure that local interest rates track US rates steadily upwards over the coming two years. The Central Bank also has access to a substantial foreign asset stock, which it would use in the unlikely event that the peg came under real strain.

External sector outlook

We expect export revenue to reach a total of US$83.4 billion this year – an all-time high for the third year in succession. The performance largely reflects further expansion in energy earnings as rising prices are compounded by increases in volumes, although we also expect non-oil exports and re-exports to show growth.

Revenue will ease by around 2 per cent in 2006 as oil prices soften, but at US$81.7 billion it will remain very high by historical standards. Import spending will continue to grow strongly, rising by an average of around 10 per cent a year to reach US$54.2 billion in 2005 and US$59 billion in 2006 compared with an estimated US$48.8 billion in 2004.

The trends will be driven primarily by robust local demand for industrial and consumer goods as well as by demand for re-exports. Some pick-up in euro-denominated average non-oil prices is also likely. Overall, we forecast that this will leave the UAE with a trade surplus of US$29.2 billion in 2005 (the equivalent of 30.5 per cent of GDP), an increase of around US$3.3 billion on the previous year. We expect the surplus to narrow but remain very large in 2006 at US$22.6 billion.

Services earnings are expected to strengthen over the forecast period, driven largely by further growth in the tourism sector, although commercial services are also projected to expand. Income credits, too, will rise as higher international interest rates boost the return on the emirates' stock of foreign assets, the overall value of which will continue to grow in line with the large external account surpluses anticipated over the forecast period. These inflows will be more than offset, however, by large non-merchandise outflows, which will be dominated by services debits associated with the industrialization programme and rising import volumes.

Income debits will also strengthen as debt-service payments pick up in line with international interest rates and the profits of foreign firms rise, particularly those working in the oil sector. The expatriate workforce will continue to grow, ensuring that remittance outflows remain high. Overall, we believe this will leave the UAE with a current-account surplus of US$14.8 billion (15.4 per cent of GDP) in 2005 compared with US$12.4 billion in 2004. The surplus is forecast to narrow to a still-large US$8.3 billion (9.1 per cent of GDP) in 2006.

Table 1.2.4. UAE outlook for 2005–06 (forecast)

	2003[a]	**2004[b]**	**2005[c]**	**2006[c]**
Real GDP growth	7.0	5.9	6.8	6.4
Oil production ('000 barrels/day)	2,290	2,353[a]	2,462	2,525
Crude oil exports (US$ million)	22,113	28,744	34,923	31,678
Consumer price inflation (average)	3.1	3.6	3.3	3.0
Deposit rate	1.2	1.6	3.4	4.7
Government balance (% of GDP)	−4.6	−0.7	−0.5	−4.5
Exports of goods fob (US$ billion)	60.8	74.7	83.4	81.7
Imports of goods fob (US$ billion)	41.7	48.8	54.2	59.0
Current-account balance (US$ billion)	6.8	12.4	14.8	8.3
Current-account balance (% of GDP)	8.5	13.8	15.4	9.1
External debt (year-end; US$ billion)	22.7[b]	26.0	28.4	30.5
Exchange rate dirham:US dollar (average)	3.67	3.67[a]	3.67	3.67

Source: EIU

1.3

Dubai's Economy and Foreign Trade Environment

Data Management and Business Research Department, DCCI

Introduction

Dubai is distinguished as one of the trade centres in the Arabian Gulf region. It has acquired this position for several reasons, which can be summarized as follows:

- It occupies a strategic competitive location in the middle of the UAE coast, stretching along 400 miles. This distinguished location in the southwestern part of the Arabian Gulf enabled it to play an active trading role in linking maritime lines and transporting goods between East and West easily.
- Pursuing free and balanced economic policy supported the distinguished strategic location of Dubai. This policy shaped the good reputation of Dubai in the international, commercial and economic communities. Therefore, national and foreign capitals were encouraged to enter into successful investment ventures in different commercial, industrial and services fields.
- Setting up the state-of-the-art infrastructure, services and utilities in Dubai has not only highlighted the importance of its strategic location but also encouraged the free economic policy. These facilities have been put into operation with high efficiency. As a result, an immediate and positive impact was reflected in the growth rates of the economic sectors, social development and improvement in living standards.

In general, the economy of Dubai is based on three main activities: non-oil trade, oil producing and exporting. During the last three decades, Dubai has witnessed a big improvement in the growth rates in trade and industrial activities due to the strategic location and the state-of-the-art infrastructure. This helped the emirate to become one of the largest centres of import, export and re-export in the region.

During the last two decades, Dubai has tended to enhance the industrial base, aiming at the diversification of the sources of income. Therefore, heavy industrial projects were established in the Jebel Ali free zone; on the other hand, the active private sector has contributed to setting up medium and small manufacturing industries. This, to some extent, resulted in self-sufficiency in some of the consumer products that may exceed the purpose of being exported to overseas markets. Table 1.3.1 shows the development of the value of the Dubai's GDP at the cost of production factors between 2000 and 2003.

Table 1.3.1. Dubai GDP at current prices by economic sector 2000–03 (AED million)

Sectors	2000	2001	2002	2003*
Non-financial corporations	*51,681*	*54,188*	*57,994*	*63,190*
Agriculture, livestock and fishing	501	525	544	655
Mining and quarrying:	6,443	5,142	5,003	5,468
Crude oil and natural gas	6,365	5,068	4,926	5,385
Quarrying	78	74	77	83
Manufacturing industries	10,090	10,538	11,174	12,171
Electricity, gas and water	1,031	1,080	1,133	1,190
Construction	5,066	5,218	5,378	5,724
Wholesale, retail, trade and repairing services	10,163	10,517	11,405	12,202
Restaurants and hotels	2,713	2,977	3,243	3,475
Transports, storage and communication	8,047	10,211	11,783	13,519
Real estate and business services	6,057	6,290	6,514	6,863
Social and personal services	1,570	1,690	1,817	1,923
Financial corporations	*6,187*	*7,517*	*7,992*	*8,498*
Government services	*5,659*	*5,939*	*6,735*	*6,905*

Sectors	2000	2001	2002	2003*
Domestic household services	475	567	598	598
Less: imputed bank services	1,667	2,183	2,572	2,733
Total	62,335	66,028	70,747	76,458

*preliminary

Source: Ministry of Planning

Dubai foreign trade

During previous years, foreign trade in Dubai was very active. It achieved a considerable rise in the rates of trade exchange growth locally, regionally and internationally. The active movement was a reflection of the requirements of the local and regional markets covered by trading channels that are the free import of most consumable, intermediate and capital goods. Table 1.3.2 shows the development of Dubai's non-oil foreign trade in weight and value during 1999–2003.

Nature of commodity exports (non-oil) and their geographical distribution

Dubai takes the lead among the other emirates in the volume of exports; its exports constitute around 78.4 per cent of the country's total exports. The non-oil exports consist of two main groups. The first consists of the export of traditional commodities that include dates, hides, frozen and dried fish, iron scrap and other metals. This group represents a minor percentage of the total exports value, most of which is directed to the Gulf states and the countries of the Indian subcontinent. The second group is the export of manufacturing industries that are imported by the Arabian Gulf countries and other international markets.

Dubai exports aluminium ingots, liquefied gas and ready-made garments to the USA, South Korea, Japan, UK, Netherlands, India, Taiwan, China and some industrial countries in Western Europe. The Arab Gulf Cooperation Council (GCC) markets consume most of the remaining UAE exports from manufactured commodities such as foodstuffs, chemicals, plastic products, building materials and metallic products. It is noticeable that Dubai's exports of traditional agricultural commodities or modern manufactured goods are minimal. Nevertheless, it is hoped that Dubai's exports of manufactured goods,

Table 1.3.2. Development of Dubai's total non-oil foreign trade by value and weight (1999–2003)

Year	Imports		Exports		Re-exports		Total (non-oil) foreign trade	
	Weight (Kg)	Value (AED)	Weight (Kg)	Value (AED)	Weight (Kg)	Value (AED)	Weight (Kg)	Value (AED)
1999	11,195,666,230	65,604,746,673	1,399,491,278	5,127,590,099	2,155,031,737	15,030,754,691	14,750,189,245	85,763,091,463
2000	11,037,449,249	72,392,454,378	1,347,197,330	5,463,992,895	2,372,514,854	17,659,184,234	14,757,161,433	95,515,631,507
2001	11,428,300,367	83,186,850,042	1,569,617,375	5,909,284,687	2,464,973,010	22,575,373,861	15,462,890,752	111,671,508,590
2002	12,713,332,469	90,257,037,916	2,192,775,504	6,377,923,681	3,394,489,780	29,615,925,905	18,300,597,753	126,250,887,502
2003	15,532,842,746	108,734,695,717	2,800,384,683	6,581,561,698	3,727,236,975	37,748,393,852	22,060,464,404	153,064,651,267

Source: Dubai Ports, Customs and Free Zone Corporation

such as aluminium ingots, liquefied gas, cement, electric cables and others, will increase in the near future due to the expansion of the industrial activity in the country.

Table 1.3.3 shows the development of the value of Dubai's exports as per the harmonized system for commodity classification and coding during 2002–03.

Table 1.3.3. Development of Dubai's exports 2002–03 (AED million)

Rank	Data Harmonized System	2002	2003	% change
1	Live animals; animal products	91	91	0.0
2	Vegetable products	59	107	81.4
3	Animal/vegetable fats and oil; prepared edible fats; waxes	129	118	−8.5
4	Prepared foodstuffs; beverages; spirits and vinegar; tobacco and manufactured tobacco substitutes	429	792	84.6
5	Mineral products	352	428	21.6
6	Products of chemicals and allied industries	353	388	9.9
7	Plastics and articles thereof; rubber and articles thereof	280	301	7.5
8	Raw hides and skins; leather; fur-skins and articles thereof; saddlery and harness; travel goods; handbags and similar containers; articles of animal gut (other than silk-worm gut)	24	16	−33.3
9	Wood and articles of wood; wood charcoal; cork and articles of cork; manufactures of straw, esparto or other plaiting materials; basketware and wickerwork	1	2	100.0
10	Pulp of wood or other fibrous cellulosic material; waste and scrap of paper or paperboard; paper and paperboard and articles thereof	157	150	−4.5
11	Textiles and textile articles	733	641	−12.6
12	Footwear; headgear; umbrellas; parasols; walking sticks; seatsticks; whips; riding crops and parts thereof; prepared feathers and articles made therewith; artificial flowers; articles of human hair	6	4	−33.3
13	Articles of stones; plaster; cement; asbestos; mica or similar materials; ceramic products; glass and glassware	433	468	8.1

Rank	Data Harmonized System	2002	2003	% change
14	Natural or cultured pearls; precious or semi-precious stones; precious metals; metals clad with precious metal and articles thereof; imitation jewellery; coins	120	32	−73.3
15	Base metals and articles of base metals	3,047	2,881	−5.4
16	Machinery and mechanical appliances; electrical equipment; parts thereof	67	70	4.5
17	Vehicles, aircraft, vessels and associated transport equipment	17	16	−5.9
18	Optical, photographic, cinematographic, measuring, checking, precision, medical or surgical instruments and apparatus; clocks and watches; musical instruments; parts and accessories thereof	1	1	0.0
19	Arms and ammunition; parts and accessories thereof	0	0	0.0
20	Miscellaneous manufactured articles	81	77	−4.9
21	Works of arts; collectors' pieces; antiques	0	0	0.0
Total		**6,380**	**6,583**	**3.2**

Source: Dubai Ports, Customs and Free Zone Corporation

As to the geographical distribution of Dubai commodity exports, USA occupied the first place in 2003 with a share of 6.7 per cent of Dubai's total exports. Table 1.3.4 shows the development of the value of Dubai's exports and the share of each country in the total exports during 2002–03.

Table 1.3.4. Development of the value of Dubai's exports and major importing countries 2002–03 (AED million)

Country	2002	Rank	Country	2003	Rank
USA	575	1	USA	440	1
Japan	545	2	Japan	427	2
South Korea	405	3	India	416	3
India	320	4	Iran	347	4
Netherlands	286	5	South Korea	316	5
UK	282	6	Kuwait	283	6

Country	2002	Rank	Country	2003	Rank
Iran	266	7	Netherlands	255	7
China	212	8	UK	235	8
Yemen	210	9	Taiwan	234	9
Kuwait	195	10	Yemen	228	10
Others	3,082	–	Others	3,402	–
Total	**6,378**	**–**	**Total**	**6,583**	**–**

Source: Dubai Ports, Customs and Free Zone Corporation

Nature of commodity imports (non-oil) and their geographical distribution

The volume and value of Dubai's annual imports are important indicators of all commercial activities in the UAE. This is because Dubai imports more than two-thirds of the UAE requirements of all kinds of consumable, intermediatory and capital goods, in addition to a part of the requirements of the GCC countries.

The (non-oil) commodity imports of Dubai registered an increasing growth amounting to 20.5 per cent during 2002–03 when the value of these imports reached AED108,735 million in 2003 against AED72,392 million in 2002. Table 1.3.5 shows the development of Dubai's imports as per the harmonized system for commodity classification and coding during 2002–03.

Table 1.3.5. Development of the value of Dubai's imports 2002–03 (AED million)

Rank	Data Harmonized System	2002	2003	% change
1	Live animals; animal products	1,570	1,699	8.2
2	Vegetable products	3,597	3,683	2.4
3	Animal/vegetable fats and oil; prepared edible fats; waxes	258	305	18.2
4	Prepared foodstuffs; beverages; spirits and vinegar; tobacco and manufactured tobacco substitutes	2,411	3,860	60.1
5	Mineral products	623	903	44.9
6	Products of chemicals and allied industries	5,027	6,201	23.4

Rank	Data Harmonized System	2002	2003	% change
7	Plastics and articles thereof; rubber and articles thereof	3,227	3,836	18.9
8	Raw hides and skins; leather; fur-skins and articles thereof; saddlery and harness; travel goods; handbags and similar containers; articles of animal gut (other than silk-worm gut)	520	544	4.6
9	Wood and articles of wood; wood charcoal; cork and articles of cork; manufactures of straw, esparto or of other plaiting materials; basket-ware and wickerwork	869	1046	20.4
10	Pulp of wood or other fibrous cellulosic material; waste and scrap of paper or paperboard; paper and paperboard and articles thereof	1,016	1,152	13.4
11	Textiles and textile articles	9,597	10,457	9.0
12	Footwear; headgear; umbrellas; parasols; walking-sticks; seat-sticks; whips; riding crops and parts thereof; prepared feathers and articles made therewith; artificial flowers; articles made of human hair	973	1,051	8.0
13	Articles of stones; plaster; cement; asbestos; mica or similar materials; ceramic products; glass and glassware	1,877	2,133	13.6
14	Natural or cultured pearls; precious or semi-precious stones; precious metals; metals clad with precious metal and articles thereof; imitation jewellery; coins	17,196	20,232	17.7
15	Base metals and articles of base metal	5,963	7,697	29.1
16	Machinery and mechanical appliances; electrical equipment; parts thereof	20,509	23,202	13.1
17	Vehicles; aircraft; vessels and associated transport equipment	9,730	14,940	53.5
18	Optical, photographic, cinematographic, measuring, checking, precision, medical or surgical instruments and apparatus; clocks and watches; musical instruments; parts and accessories thereof	2,667	2,813	5.5
19	Arms and ammunition; parts and accessories thereof	7	11	57.1

Rank	Data Harmonized System	2002	2003	% change
20	Miscellaneous manufactured articles	2,609	2,960	13.5
21	Works of arts; collectors' pieces; antiques	12	10	−16.7
Total		**90,258**	**108,735**	**20.5**

Source: Dubai Ports, Customs and Free Zone Corporation

During 2003, Dubai imported from 166 countries all over the world, the most important of which were China, UK, Japan, India, USA, Switzerland, Germany, France, South Korea and Italy. The share of all these countries in Dubai's total imports amounted to 64.9 per cent of the total imports. Table 1.3.6 shows the development of Dubai's imports by main countries and the share of each country in the total imports during 2002–03.

Table 1.3.6. Development of the value of Dubai's imports value by main countries 2002–03 (AED million)

Country	2002	Rank	Country	2003	Rank
China	10,593	1	China	13,312	1
Japan	6,766	2	India	9,638	2
India	6,566	3	Japan	8,253	3
USA	6,556	4	Germany	7,088	4
Germany	5,845	5	USA	6,832	5
UK	5,622	6	France	6,568	6
South Korea	5,033	7	UK	5,989	7
Switzerland	4,536	8	South Korea	4,384	8
France	3,884	9	Switzerland	4,302	9
Italy	3,770	10	Italy	4,220	10
Others	31,086	–	Others	38,159	–
Total	**90,257**	**–**	**Total**	**108,735**	**–**

Nature of re-exported commodities and their geographical distribution

Over its long commercial history, Dubai has been well known as an active centre for re-export trade to neighbouring Gulf countries, and even to the Indian subcontinent and the eastern coast of Africa. Dubai has recently been able to invest its own abilities and take advantage of its several distinctive characteristics and the diversified facilities to expand its re-export activities to cover all the Gulf and Arab countries and countries of Asia, Europe, the Americas and some African countries.

The re-export trade in Dubai plays an important role in its foreign trade as its share amounted to 24.6 per cent of its total foreign trade in 2003. The total value of re-export trade of Dubai amounted to AED37,750 million in 2003. Table 1.3.7 shows the development of Dubai's re-exports as per the harmonized system for commodity classification and coding during 2002 and 2003.

Table 1.3.7. Development of Dubai's re-exports 2002–03 (AED million)

Rank	Data Harmonized System	2002	2003	% change
1	Live animals; animal products	203	279	37.4
2	Vegetable products	1,453	1,478	1.7
3	Animal/vegetable fats and oil; prepared edible fats; waxes	29	50	72.4
4	Prepared foodstuff; beverages; spirits and vinegar; tobacco andmanufactured tobacco substitutes	925	1,289	39.4
5	Mineral products	73	114	56.2
6	Products of chemicals and allied industries	1,243	1,439	15.8
7	Plastics and articles thereof; rubber and articles thereof	1,111	1,331	19.8
8	Raw hides and skins; leather, fur-skins and articles thereof, saddleryand harness, travel goods, handbags, and similar containers, articlesof animal gut, (other than silk-worm gut)	177	240	35.6
9	Wood and articles of wood, wood charcoal, cork and articles of cork, manufactures of straw, of esparato or of other plaiting materials, basket-ware and wickerwork	140	200	42.9
10	Pulp of wood or other fibrous cellulosic material, waste and scrap of paper or paperboard, paper and paperboard and articles thereof	161	176	9.3
11	Textiles and textile articles	4,221	4,949	17.2

Rank	Data Harmonized System	2002	2003	% change
12	Footwear, headgear, umbrellas, sun umbrellas, walking-sticks, seat-sticks, whips, riding crops and parts thereof, prepared feathers and articles made therewith, artificial flowers, articles made of human hair	318	485	52.5
13	Articles of stones, plaster, cement, asbestos, mica or similar materials, ceramic products, glass and glassware	831	1,110	33.6
14	Natural or cultured pearls, precious or semi-precious stones, precious metals, metals clad with precious metal and articles thereof, imitation jewellery, coin	4,638	7,689	65.8
15	Base metals and articles of base metal	1,560	1,790	14.7
16	Machinery and mechanical appliances, electrical equipment, parts thereof	7,938	9,407	18.5
17	Vehicles, aircraft, vessels and associated transport equipment	2,642	3,616	36.9
18	Optical, photographic, cinematographic, measuring, checking, precision, medical or surgical instruments and apparatus; clocks and watches; musical instruments; parts and accessories thereof	710	804	13.2
19	Arms and ammunition; parts and accessories thereof	2	3	50.0
20	Miscellaneous manufactured articles	1,235	1,300	5.3
21	Works of arts, collectors' pieces, antiques.	4	1	−75.0
Total		**29,614**	**37,750**	**27.4**

Source: Dubai Ports, Customs and Free Zone Corporation

Destinations of Dubai re-exports totaled 198 countries – the most important of them are Iran, India, Switzerland, Iraq, Pakistan, UK, Saudi Arabia, Algeria, Libya and Kuwait. The total value of goods re-exported to these countries amounted to AED22,146 million in 2003 or 58.6 per cent of the value of re-exported goods. Table 1.3.8 shows the development of Dubai re-exports by main countries and the share of each country during 2002 and 2003.

Table 1.3.8. Development of Dubai's re-export value by main countries 2002–03 (AED million)

Country	2002	Rank	Country	2003	Rank
Iran	7,399	1	Iran	7,838	1
India	2,229	2	India	3,028	2
Iraq	1,768	3	Switzerland	2,150	3
Saudi Arabia	1,344	4	Iraq	2,062	4
Pakistan	1,079	5	Pakistan	1,533	5
Libya	1,034	6	UK	1,199	6
Kuwait	875	7	Saudi Arabia	1,192	7
Switzerland	783	8	Algeria	1,145	8
Algeria	759	9	Libya	1,130	9
USA	710	10	Kuwait	869	10
Others	11,634	–	Others	15,604	–
Total	**29,614**	**–**	**Total**	**37,750**	**–**

Source: Dubai Ports, Customs and Free Zone Corporation

Appendix 1:

Oil and its role in the economic development of Dubai

The economic activity in Dubai depended on transit trade, pearl fishing, fishing, livestock and on a small quantity of agricultural products. As a result of the flourishing of the pearl trade, in addition to other commercial activities practised in Dubai over centuries, the emirate was known as 'The Pearl of the Gulf'. However, with the flow of cheap cultured and artificial pearls, natural pearls had become a part of history. What is left of this industry is the reputation linked with the pearl trade, which is still standing as it was in ancient times.

Oil discovery

On 6 June 1966, and after three years of drilling and exploration works undertaken by Dubai Petroleum Company, oil was discovered for the first time. The 6 September 1969 was officially declared as the beginning of oil production in the offshore Fatah well. In May 1982 the discovery of Morghem Well was declared; this was the first onshore oil well located 40km from Dubai city.

Commercial quantities of gas were also discovered in these wells. A big complex for processing and liquefying gas was established to utilize this gas for industrial purposes. The complex was opened in 1980 to process 130 million cubic feet of gas per day.

The role of oil in development

The sources of Dubai's income have been diversified with the export of oil. In addition to the traditional trade, oil and liquefied gas have formed the biggest share of the income. The other non-oil sources, such as industrial production, have formed one of the essential sources of income. No doubt, the discovery of oil and its export were a turning point because many big achievements in different areas have been realized within a few years as a result of oil wealth availability.

The oil sector is considered the most significant economic factor in Dubai – despite the medium level of oil production, oil revenues enabled the emirate to achieve development in all areas at rapid speed. This included infrastructural as well as industrial, sanitary, services, housing and education projects. The construction of the infrastructure in Dubai has started on a modern basis in order to provide it with all utilities needed; this was the reason for the sudden inflow of huge numbers of manpower as well as capital for the establishment of investment projects in the emirate.

1.4

Market Research in the UAE

Jan Stuffers, Managing Consultant,
InCite Research & Marketing Solutions

The UAE market

Few would argue that when it comes to business, the UAE is one of the most exciting markets in the Gulf region. The country's per capita GDP among the Gulf Cooperation Council (GCC) nations ranks second after Qatar and is on a par with European countries such as Germany and France. The pace of development is dazzling, as is evident to any visitor witnessing the myriad of construction sites along the coastline of Dubai, from which sprout high-rise buildings and luxury villa communities. Large construction projects are similarly under way in many of the other six emirates that, along with Dubai, make up the UAE. These are signals of a flourishing economy that, over the years, has relied less and less on oil revenues. Progressive government policies have been effective in attracting overseas investment, elevating the status of the UAE to that of *the* business hub for the Arabian Peninsula and beyond.

Unique to the UAE is also its demographic composition with nationals only accounting for around 20 per cent of the population. The expatriate community is richly diverse with large helpings from Asia, other Middle Eastern countries and, to a lesser extent, Europe. Such a 'pot pourri' of cultures in the setting of a rapidly developing economy is an exciting challenge to any market research practitioner. Understanding consumers across different countries is complex enough; making sense of research drawn from different nationalities in the *same* country demands not only expertise in selecting the right research technique, but also a thorough understanding of the different lifestyles and mindsets of the various nationality groups across socioeconomic classes. In short, this is not just number-crunching but also involves adding context to research findings from a cultural perspective.

Why research?

Generally, just under 65 per cent of new businesses fail within their first three years and as many as 86 per cent of new brands suffer the same fate. Listening to customers – be they prospective or existing – and adapting to their constantly changing wants and needs is critical in maintaining, as well as creating, excitement and demand for products or services. Market research can definitely help maximize the potential of initiatives, no matter what the area of the marketing mix; likewise it can prevent costly misjudgements by bridging the perilous cleft between the marketer's perceptions and the reality of market dynamics. This applies to any idea – a new business, changing or developing new (service) products, advertising, packaging etc – that demands precious investment of a company's time and capital.

Multinationals operating in the region – especially manufacturers of fast-moving consumer goods – have always used market research in a bid to sharpen their competitive edge and grow their markets. Now large local and regional companies are complementing sharp business instincts with market insights and have, for this reason, taken a keener interest in market research. Indeed, the research business is growing by some 12 per cent per annum. According to ESOMAR, the expenditure on market research in the GCC stood at US$51 million in 2004.

Primary market research (interviews)

Most statistical analyses used in consumer research are based on the concept of random sampling. For cultural and religious reasons this sampling technique in quantitative (numeric) research is, at best, difficult and, in most cases, impossible. Research agencies usually resort to a method based on referrals to achieve a required number of interviews, but this inevitably leads to an inherent bias. Various techniques are used to minimize this effect, but it cannot be completely eradicated. Similarly, in arranging focus groups, great care needs to be taken with the composition of respondents and the choice of the moderator. Mixing gender for Emirati groups is not only counter-productive, but is considered embarrassing and offensive.

Good researchers understand, respect and accommodate in their research practice the sensitivities of different lifestyles, especially when driven by Islamic or ethnic values. Nationals in particular are hospitable and this helps the researcher to find willing respondents.

However, cordiality may extend into providing overly accommodating answers. The gap between what is said and what is actually done is influenced by the culture of the respondent. It is generally wider with Arabs and Asians compared with Westerners. This phenomenon is especially of concern when the research is designed to predict intended behaviour, for example when attempts are made, as part of a feasibility or market entry survey, to predict potential demand for a product or service that may not even exist yet. Answers from respondents cannot always be taken at face value.

Face-to-face personal interviews are still the norm in collecting data and offer good quality, especially when the topic is complex. Such sessions should not exceed 25 minutes – beyond this duration the quality of answers deteriorates rapidly. Computer-aided telephone interviewing (CATI) has gained popularity because of its cost efficiency and speed of turnaround, but interviewing time should not exceed 10 minutes. Historically, telephone interviews have been more common in business-to-business research, but they are increasingly also used for consumer surveys. Internet self-completion questionnaires – in whatever form – are also gaining ground, but there are lingering concerns about how representative samples are, since not all residents have access to the net. Nonetheless, for selected consumer segments, internet research is moving forward.

Some of the more common surveys that research agencies handle are given in Figure 1.4.1.

Continuous multiclient surveys, such as retail audits and media-tracking services, have been available for many years. Their findings are mostly relevant to multinational manufacturing companies marketing fast-moving consumer goods. The retail-based audits provide brand share, distribution and allied data on consumer goods and are a useful tool in monitoring the development of brands in terms of demand and retail visibility. Some manufacturing companies and advertising agencies also subscribe to tracking studies for consumer media habits to help optimize their advertising spend. There are other syndicated and continuous surveys operated by various research agencies with the aim of offering regular market research data cost effectively.

Secondary market research (published data)

When considering doing business in any country, companies need statistics that provide a basic understanding of the potential the market can offer. The population size with a demographic analysis is the most obvious requirement. Reliable import and export data, together with economic indicators such as GDP and information regarding

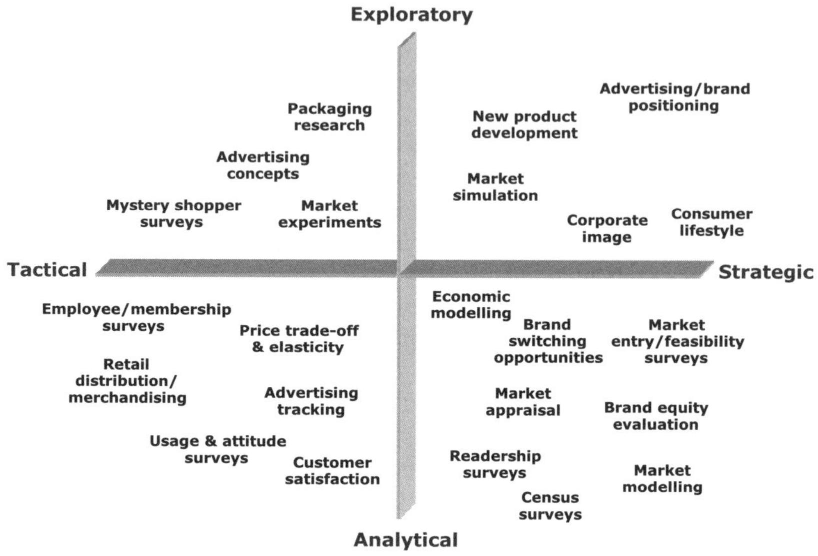

Figure 1.4.1. Common market research surveys

domestic household expenditure are other useful guidelines a marketer keenly uses when considering market entry or development.

However, even specialist market research agencies operating in the Gulf find it difficult to source reliable secondary data for most GCC states, let alone companies based overseas that are less familiar with the region. Although census surveys among the UAE's population are conducted, not all details are in the public domain; as an example, there are no confirmed figures regarding the origins of the various expatriate segments. There is no income tax in the emirates and, therefore, statistics regarding socioeconomic classes are absent. Other useful information sources such as import and export figures are available for Dubai and Abu Dhabi, but are much harder to come by in the remaining emirates. It has to be said that the available information is improving in quantity and quality, but sourcing secondary research still remains one of the most challenging tasks to research agencies.

Market research agencies

There are about a dozen professional research companies in the UAE. An encouraging sign of the growing market research industry is the emergence of smaller and medium-sized research agencies in addition to well-known international research groups. Selecting the right agency can present a leap of faith, especially with local or regional operators. Selecting an ESOMAR-registered agency (see www.esomar.org) offers the best reassurance on standards. ESOMAR is a global organization of research practitioners and it sets out as concisely as possible the basic ethical and business principles that govern the practice of marketing and social research. It specifies the rules that are to be followed in dealing with the general public and the business community, including clients and other members of the profession. Big research spenders generally insist on using ESOMAR-registered agencies.

Most research companies in the UAE are full service agencies offering both qualitative and quantitative expertise. Essentially, qualitative research – eg focus groups – is exploratory in nature, often used to generate ideas and to fully probe (mostly) consumers' attitudes. Quantitative research adds a numeric perspective by interviewing large numbers of respondents with a structured questionnaire. Understanding is gained through measurement. Larger international research groups offer a wider range of proprietary research models for in-depth analysis. These are primarily designed for the needs of multinational clients to monitor their brand or advertising performance.

Although the research industry is growing, the market is still too small for agencies to focus only on one particular industry. As such, most conduct research in a variety of business sectors. Against this backdrop it pays to find out what experience an agency has in a particular business stream.

The adage 'rubbish in, rubbish out' is the hot potato of the research industry; no matter how slick a report might be, bad fieldwork inevitably leads to misleading recommendations. With due diligence, ESOMAR-registered agencies employ a number of quality control procedures to safeguard the quality of data collection. Typical procedures for field operations include full logic checking of completed questionnaires and back-checking a random sample (minimum of 30 per cent) of interviews.

Dealing with agencies in the UAE

Research briefs submitted by prospective clients to agencies range from multiple pages to one-liners. Generally speaking, the crisper the brief, the better the proposal in response. A clear definition of the objectives is the more critical aspect leaving some space for the agency to recommend the level of information needed and how this should be gathered to meet the objectives. From the content of the proposal, prospective research buyers can easily judge the expertise of the agency. Some basic principles to follow include:

- A written briefing is a must: have one and list objectives in bullet points, eg demographic and geographic description of the target market.
- Without having to share the budget, it is worth asking informally the likely cost of running the type of survey considered. This will help set some parameters for the agency and avoids receiving a proposal that is well off-budget.
- Ask the agency to specify its experience in the relevant line of business.
- Enquire about resources; for example the number of full-time research consultants, their experience, number of interviewers and other company credentials such as clients.
- Visit the agency's offices. This can be an eye-opener.
- Ask about quality-control procedures, training of interviewers and verification of their work.
- Ask to see some examples of reports.
- If time allows, insist on attending briefings and selected interviews.
- Request regular updates on sample progress.

Although research in the UAE is less expensive compared with the USA, Western European countries and Japan (mostly because of lower rates in human resources), striking a close working relationship with the agency – which is something that researchers tend to prefer – inevitably leads to a better return from the investment.

Part Two

Banking, Finance and Investments

2.1

UAE Monetary Policy and the Role of the Central Bank

Data Management and Business Research Department, DCCI

Introduction

The banking system in the UAE consists of the Central Bank; national and foreign commercial banks; development institutions; the industrial and finance bank; investment banks and financial investment companies; finance companies; banking, financial and investment consultancy companies; exchange bureaus; brokers and banks' representatives offices.

The Central Bank of the UAE

Major developments were witnessed by the economic activity after the formation of the federation and the tremendous developments of the banking and financial sector at both local and international levels. Such developments resulted in an overlapping among the activities of the commercial banks and the other financial institutions. Therefore, there was an urgent need to change the currency board, which was established in 1973, into a Central Bank to perform all the ordinary functions of the central bank.

On 2 August 1980 the Federal Law No. 10 concerning the central bank, the monetary system and the organization of banking was issued. This came into force on 10 December 1980 when the UAE Central Bank was established to replace the currency board. The new law vested in the Central Bank all powers that were missed by the currency board in order to apply a proper and effective banking and credit policy. This endeavour was intended to enable it to support financial stability and thereby unite the foundation of the banking system in the country.

Article 5 of the law defined the main objects of the Central Bank as organizing monetary, credit and banking policy, and supervising its implementation in accordance with the general policy of the UAE to support the national economy and stabilize its currency. In order to attain these objectives, the same article authorized the Central Bank to perform the following functions.

Exercising the privilege of currency issue in accordance with the provisions of the law

This includes the issue of bank notes and coins of various denominations determined by the law; providing different economic sectors in the state, through the commercial banks, with their requirements of bank notes and coins; maintaining stock of bank notes to meet future requirements of the economic sectors; replacing bank notes and destroying the damaged ones; compensating and exchanging the damaged bank notes; handling counterfeiting cases of the circulated currency and issuing commemorative coins.

Endeavouring to support the currency, maintaining its stability internally and externally, and ensuring its free convertibility into foreign currencies

It was of utmost importance to pursue a flexible policy for the local currency exchange rate that complies with the demands of the economy. The following were among the most outstanding aspects that were taken into consideration while deciding those policies:

1. Dependence of the local economy, in general, and the government budget in particular on all revenues, which are paid in US dollars.
2. The rise in the rate of imports and the importance of imports to the local economy together with their sources, price levels and the effect of this on the rate of inflation in the country.
3. Surplus of the trading account, current account and the huge investments abroad, especially in the US economy.
4. The UAE compliance, as a member of OPEC, with decisions in respect of the quotas and oil prices.
5. Continuous commitment of the state to coordinate its monetary policies with the Gulf Cooperation Council (GCC) countries.

6. The freedom enjoyed by the local economy as a result of applying free-market policies.
7. The low non-oil exports rate, which cannot be raised by changing the exchange rate of the dirham.

The exchange rate policy in the UAE witnessed many changes during the period of the currency board in accordance with the changes witnessed by world financial markets. In the early 1970s, the dirham was linked with the US dollar with a narrow fluctuation margin not exceeding 1 per cent. Later on, the dirham was linked with the special drawing rights (SDR) in a central exchange rate of AED4.7619 for every unit of the SDR with a fluctuated margin of 2.25 per cent up and down around the central linkage rate. Then, this margin was widened to 7.25 per cent. Although the rate of the dirham is related to the SDR, the US dollar remained, representing the mediator currency used by the bank to maintain these transactions with the state. In 1980, the dirham was raised against the US dollar to become AED3.671 for each dollar as a mediator.

The UAE Central Bank has adopted the policy of continuous coordination with the monetary authorities and the central banks of the GCC states – not only in the currencies exchange rate but also on all monetary policies such as budget balance, foreign reserves, public debt, interest rates on deposits and inflation.

Ensuring free exchange of the local currency to foreign currencies

The Central Bank strives to ensure a free exchange of the local currency to foreign currencies. The bank has met all the requirements of the banks and financial, monetary and international institutions to exchange dirham into dollars.

Ratio of currency cover

In order to support the dirham and maintain its value domestically and abroad, the Central Bank maintained a high level of the ratio of currency cover in circulation outside the bank and demand deposits. In accordance with the law, the ratio of the currency cover should always consist of gold bullion and coins, readily and freely convertible foreign currencies in the form of demand and time deposits with banking institutions abroad, the state's holdings with the International Monetary Fund (IMF), amounts lent to the fund and holdings of special drawing rights, foreign bonds, notes and certificates issued or guaranteed by foreign governments, or by international financial or monetary institutions, provided that all such instruments are first class and are denominated in convertible currencies and readily negotiable in financial markets and that they mature within seven years from the date of purchase, as well as loans granted to the government together with the Darien-denominated commercial instruments, or loans granted to the commercial banks operating in the UAE provided that their maturity falls due within a period not to exceed six months from the date of their conclusion.

Directing the credit policy to achieve a balanced growth of the national economy

The Central Bank has undertaken several procedures and issued decisions aiming to control the cost and amount of credit. In addition to the procedure taken to influence the size of cashflow in banks such as determining the ratio of the compulsory reserve, compulsory reserve on lending and deposits with unresident banks, bartering facilities, free interest rate policy, issue of deposit certificates, determine the percentage of the capital compared with the total assets and personal loans conditions.

The credit facilities, including the loans granted to the members of the Board of Directors, concentrated on one or a related group of loan receivers and other influential procedures that control the amount of credits granted by banks. There are selective procedures aiming to improve the financial positions of these banks and assuring their continuous safety so that they can implement their role properly such as allocation of provisions for bad debts, establishing a risk centre to complete the information related to credit facilities of the commercial banks clients as well as regulating the issuance of cheques so as to curb the phenomena of bounced cheques.

The organization, development and control of banking system

The organization and development of banking

In this respect, the Central Bank took several measures, the most important of which were:

1. Issuance of a decree restricting and limiting the number of the branches of the foreign commercial banks.
2. The Central Bank strove to issue Law No. (6) of 1985 in respect of Islamic banks, financial investment institutions and companies. By

this law, the Central Bank was entrusted with the supervision of such banks, institutions and companies.

3. The Central Bank prepared a draft law to amend the Federal Law No. (10) of 1980.

4. The Central Bank issued the Decision No. 123/7/1992, dated 29 November 1992, including the new system for the exchange institutions and companies to cope with the growing activity of exchange, the increasing number of exchange bureaus and the increase in the volume of their transactions.

5. In order to regulate the business of the financial investment companies and enhance their practices to the standards of the protection of the investors funds as well as the goodwill of this profession in the state, the Central Bank issued Decision No. 164/8/94, dated 8 April 1995. This included the organization of the financial investment companies as well as the banking, financial and investment consultancy companies. Pursuant to this decision, the financial investment company should be a juridical person with a minimum capital of AED25 million, in accordance with the planned business by the company. In respect of the banking, financial and investment consultancy companies, the decision stipulated that the institution or the company should be a natural or juridical person with a minimum paid-up capital of AED1 million.

6. The Central Bank Decision No. 126/5/95, dated 25 June 1995, regulated the practice of brokers in selling and buying local and foreign shares and bonds for the currencies, commodities and the mediation in the monetary market operations. The decision defined the minimum capital by AED1 million, AED2 million or AED3 million in conformity with the business intended by the brokers or the intermediary company.

7. The Central Bank Decision No. 57/3/96, dated 14 April 1996, reformulated the system of the representative offices. Representative offices are offices representing foreign banks or other financial institutions in the UAE. The decision stipulated that no person shall commence operations in a representative office in the UAE before being licensed in writing from the governor based on the decision of the Board of Directors.

8. The Central Bank issued the Decision No. 58/3/96, dated 14 April 1996, amended by the Decision No. 81/4/96, dated 26 May 1996, on finance companies, which are defined as the companies established under the provisions of the Federal Law No. (8) of 1984 and any

pursuant amendments to practise one or more financing business provided that the minimum paid capital is AED35 million.

9. Notice No.13-1/957/98, dated 2 November 1998, whereby the Central Bank urged all banks to ensure strict adherence to the terms and conditions of letters of credit and letters of guarantee issued/accepted by them or any other commitments. The Central Bank earlier noticed that some banks try to avoid meeting their obligations as per the terms and conditions of the letters of credit or letters of guarantee issued/accepted by them, causing their customers to initiate legal procedures to seek injunctions. The Central Bank cautioned that it will take appropriate action against banks found not to be observant of this.

10. Circular No.20/99, dated 25 January 1999, regarding application of international accounting standards (IAS). Due to the widespread use of IAS in keeping the accounts of banks and other financial institutions, accounting disclosure under these standards have become understandable worldwide, and its implementation will most likely enhance the positions of banks operating in the UAE.

11. Circular No. 21/99, dated 22 November 1999, issued to all banks operating in the country, regards cash reserve requirements. In view of the developments surrounding banking business locally and internationally, and in order to simplify the process of calculation, the Board of Directors of the Central Bank decided to change the method of calculation of cash reserve requirements, with effect from 1 January 2000, as follows:

    i. to increase the percentage of cash reserve requirements on current, savings, call and similar accounts from 6 per cent and 8 per cent to 14 per cent so as to account for the volatile nature of these accounts;

    ii. to reduce the percentage of cash reserve requirements on fixed deposits (time deposits) from 5, 3 and 2 per cent to 1 per cent, regardless of the amount and period of the deposit, in line with the Central Bank's ongoing strategy to encourage long-term deposits. All previous circulars, decisions, directives or notices on the subject have been cancelled as per this circular.

12. In order to ensure that monies earned through illegal activities abroad are not run through the financial system in the country for the benefit of those criminals, irrespective of where the crime was committed, the Central Bank issued Regulations Concerning

Procedures of Anti-Money Laundering, as per Circular No. 24/2000 dated 14 November 2000.

The scope of the procedures included all banks, moneychangers, finance companies and other financial institutions operating in the country, as well as their respective board members and employees. The procedures also apply to the branches and subsidiaries of UAE-incorporated financial institutions operating within foreign jurisdictions where such procedures either are not applied or are only partially applied.

The Regulation addressed possible money laundering through: customers accounts, investment-related transactions, international banking and financial transactions, secured and unsecured loans, and electronic banking services. The anti-money laundering procedures prescribed as per the said Regulation became effective starting 1 December 2000.

Control of banking system efficiency

As a part of its efforts to improve the performance of the commercial banks, the Central Bank worked towards supporting the role of banking control as it is the only available way to discover the aspects of weakness and improper practices in the business of banks. The articles of association of the Central Bank have determined the objects that it should achieve. The Bank has followed several ways, such as requesting periodical statements, carrying out periodical inspections, adopting the policy of individual persuasion or issuing orders and instructions and taking other measures.

A bank for the banks operating in the country

The Central Bank renders the following services to the commercial banks:

- loans and advances;
- retention of banks' deposits;
- sale of bonds;
- sales of foreign currencies to commercial banks;
- clearing services; and
- licensing new banks and branches.

The government's bank

The Central Bank should act as a government bank, advising on monetary and financial matters, as well as holding the government's reserves of gold and foreign currencies.

The government's financial agent

The Central Bank should act as the government's financial agent with the IMF and other Arab and international institutions and funds and undertake all the transactions of the UAE with these parties.

2.2

Development of Banking and Finance: Dubai Banking and Insurance

Data Management and Business Research Department, DCCI

Banking in Dubai

Banks were established in Dubai ahead of the other emirates of the UAE. This was due to the progress achieved by the trading sector. The establishment of the British Bank of the Middle East in 1946 marked the first commercial banking activity in the emirate of Dubai. The first national commercial bank (National Bank of Dubai Ltd) was established in 1963 with joint capital. After that, several commercial banks were set up in the emirate.

The discovery of oil, its exports and the inflow of oil revenues had a great impact on the development of the banking sector. The establishment of the UAE federation in 1971 was another factor for stabilizing and consolidating it. This sector finances all economic activities including the oil sector; that is why its viability and efficiency reflect the soundness of the general economic activity.

The 1990s looked like being a decade of success for the banks in Dubai. The banking system witnessed an expansion in services in the local, regional and international market. To reach this end, huge amounts of investments were injected with great economic and political expectations. The banking sector has also undergone some changes in the past few years; initiated by the UAE Central Bank, these are directed mainly towards strengthening the sector and ensuring that the financial institutions are financially sound.

Banking in Dubai tends to be centered on a large number of private commercial companies. Dubai banks are flush with deposits. In addition, they benefit from healthy profits that have enabled them to bolster their capital bases, which help in the country's development. Clients are offered a comprehensive range of services like special forms of equipment finance, certain hedging instruments and consultancy services. Customers benefit from retail banking competition as the banks frequently come up with innovative products and offer a lot more facilities to them. Car financing is one of the most competitive areas of retail financing in Dubai. Dubai's banks also offer competitive outstanding services for clients such as ATMs, point of sales (POS), electronic switch system, SWIFT (The Society for Worldwide Interbank Financial Telecommunication) and telephone banking.

Development of the banking sector

The boom in commercial activity, together with the completion of the infrastructure in the 1960s and 1970s, led to drastic changes in all aspects of economic and social life. As a result of these changes, it was important to find proper channels to accommodate the financial resources of the state and to assist in the employment of such resources.

The commercial banks contributed effectively in this respect and operated under the supervision of the currency board from 1973 until the end of 1980 when the UAE Central Bank was established. During this period, the commercial banks tried to improve their performance and the services they rendered to the individuals, public and private establishments and trading and industrial companies with the help of the continuous encouragement and support of the official authorities. For its part, the government of Dubai used to render help together with financial and moral support to the banking sector and other financial institutions so that the efficiency of the commercial banks improved. Thus, Dubai has become the leading financial and banking centre for national and foreign establishments and companies. These establishments helped to increase the economic and commercial activity not only in the emirate, but also at the UAE level. The banks of Dubai did not confine their operations to within the UAE only, but extended to some Arab and European countries, USA as well as parts of South Asia and the Indian subcontinent, confirming that these banks were able to acquire wide experience in the banking field. This qualified them to compete in the international financial and investment markets due to their high standard of services rendered to commercial and industrial establishments.

Table 2.2.1 shows the development of banks and the financial and credit institutions in Dubai during 2001–03.

Table 2.2.1. Development of financial firms in Dubai as per activity 2001–03

Financial firms	2001	2002	2003
National banks	20	21	21
National banks' branches	324	345	367
Foreign banks	26	26	25
Foreign banks' branches	109	112	109
Representative offices	49	51	48
Licensed financial and monetary intermediaries	26	18	14
Brokers in the sale and purchase of domestic and foreign shares and bonds	5	4	4
Brokers in the sale and purchase of currencies, commodities and intermediaries in money market operations	8	6	6
Brokers dealing in local shares and currencies commodities as well as in money market transactions only	1	1	1
Brokers dealing in all financial and monetary business	3	5	7
Exchange houses:			
Head office	104	105	108
Branches	127	147	166
Financial investment companies	7	8	7
Banking, financial and investment consultations establishment and companies	9	12	11

Source: Central Bank

Money exchangers

Money exchange shops conduct the business of buying and selling local and foreign currencies, traveller's cheques and bank drafts. This type of business spread widely in Dubai as a result of the increase in commercial activity and the rise in the demand for foreign currencies because of tourism and the existence of expatriate communities. Aiming at maintaining the value of the national currency and securing the safety of the banking and financial system, the UAE Central Bank regulates the activity of these shops and supervises their operations.

Emirates Industrial Bank

After the issue of the Law No. (1) of 1982, the Emirates Industrial Bank was established as a credit bank specialized in granting industrial loans to new and existing industrial projects in an effort to achieve industrial development in the country. In addition to this, the bank prepares feasibility studies for the new industrial projects.

Possible investment opportunities in the banking sector

It may be stated that the possible investment opportunities in the finance and banking sector must originate, basically, from the policies that the Central Bank endeavours to achieve, and that operate to secure the necessary cashflow from the financial surpluses in order to finance the activities that suffer from the lack of financial resources. This is in addition to services and studies related to this sector. Therefore, some of the investment aspects may be mentioned as follows:

- establishments organizing the procedure of granting credit cards;
- offices and firms offering the necessary consultations to deal in stock markets such as shares, stocks and money markets, and which prepare, publish and distribute the related reports;
- banks' representative offices: offices established and operated in Dubai by any of the international and foreign banks through which they promote the activities of the main banks in the home country or to any of their branches in the world to facilitate contact between them and the clients.

Insurance sector

The recent expansion of insurance activity has necessitated the issuance of a law to regulate the business of this vital sector, the importance of which is not less than other economic sectors. Due to this, the Federal Law No. (9) of 1984 was issued in respect of insurance companies and agents as well as their executive regulations and all related ministerial resolutions.

The most important of these resolutions were:

- Decision No. (21) of 1985 on the conditions and procedures of inscription in the register of surveyors, loss adjusters;

- Decision No. (22) of 1985 on the conditions and procedures of inscription in the register of surveyors, loss adjusters;
- Decision No. (22) of 1985 on the conditions and procedure of inscription in the register of actuary insurance experts;
- Decision No. (23) of 1985 in respect of the organization of the profession of insurance consultancy;
- Decision No. (24) of 1985 on practising the profession of insurance brokers.

It is perhaps important to point out the various reasons that helped the spread of this activity that could be attributed to the economic stability in the country after establishing the Federal State, the enormous progress in the commercial sector and the increasing value of the fixed assets invested in different projects. This is in addition to the availability of a large base for various transport services such as modern ports, airports and roads. Some local regulations, which make insurance on certain assets compulsory, also helped the expansion of this activity.

Possible investment opportunities in the insurance sector

There are many areas and services in the insurance sector in Dubai that require specialized firms to render them, such as:

- all types of reinsurance;
- fields related to survey, loss adjusters, settlement of insurance claims, inspection of damages on the insured items as well as evaluation of the amount of damage and the compensation due to the insured;
- insurance assessments and actuarial services are specialized services related to the calculation of the periodic premiums that should be paid by the insured and the amounts payable by the insurers on the expiry of the insurance policy or when damages occur to the contracting parties, calculation of the financial interests for the various periods, calculation of life and death possibilities for the insured parties, and the setting up of insurance precautions to face future claims or the claims which were submitted but not yet settled;
- insurance brokers who play the role of the agent in insurance and reinsurance deals between the insured and the reinsurance

company on one hand and between any insurer and reinsurance company on the other hand, against a commission paid by the insurance company, which concluded the deal;

- insurance advice through qualified persons with wide scientific and practical experience in the field of clients' requirements, to advise on the suitable insurance cover and to help in preparing insurance claims against the amounts to be agreed upon with clients;
- insurance consultancy is considered necessary in matters concerning the drafting of insurance and reinsurance agreement, legal regulations of each type and for setting the legal disputes about compensation amounts payable to the insured in case of any risks;
- services of chartered accountants and auditors specialized in all types of insurance activities such as book-keeping financial accounts that show the liabilities of the insurance and reinsurance companies towards others, as well as the fixed assets being dealt with, together with preparing the final balance sheets showing the financial position of these companies and profits and losses they may incur.

Further, the role of these accountants may extend to give advice in respect of the financial investments that may be practised by the insurance companies through the financial information they possess.

2.3

The UAE Capital Markets with a Special Focus on Dubai Financial Market

Data Management and Business Research Department, DCCI

Overview of Dubai Financial Market (DFM)

DFM was established as an independent public establishment. It operates as a secondary market for trading shares issued by public companies; bonds issued by the federal government, any local government, establishment or company; investment funds issued by investment companies; and any other local or foreign security acceptable by Emirates Securities and Commodities Authority (ESCA) and DFM. It commenced operations on 26 March 2000 and was inaugurated by His Highness Sheikh Mohammed bin Rashid Al Maktoum. DFM is located in the Dubai World Trade Centre in Dubai.

The aim in establishing DFM is to create a fair, efficient and transparent marketplace capable of serving the national interest. Its establishment comes as a necessary step in the completion of the financial sector's infrastructure. It supports the nation's position as a regional and international financial centre. To achieve its mission, DFM strives to achieve the following objectives:

1. to provide the opportunity to invest in securities in a manner that better serves the national economy;
2. to regulate the process of buying and selling securities, ensuring the protection of investors from unfair and improper practices;

3. to collect data and statistics about traded securities and issue reports based on this information;
4. to create liquidity in the marketplace through the interaction of supply and demand based on fair and equitable trading practices between investors;
5. to organize the transfer of ownership of securities by operating a central clearing, depository and settlement (CDS) department, which operates an electronic state-of-the-art system ensuring efficiency and timeliness of transfers;
6. to implement rules of professional conduct and discipline between brokers and DFM staff to maintain a high level of integrity and provide them with proper training;
7. to collect data and statistics about traded securities and issue reports based on this information.

DFM is governed by the rules and regulations of ESCA. In addition to ESCA's regulations, DFM has also prepared implementation regulations covering listing, disclosure and transparency, brokers, trading and clearing.

DFM is equipped with state-of-the-art technology that facilitates the liquidity of funds for the purpose of investing in securities by ensuring the interaction between supply and demand to obtain the real market values of securities. It also has an electronic system that ensures the timeliness and efficiency in the transfer of security ownership. DFM trading activity is overseen by a compliance department, which combines local market awareness and international securities market expertise.

DFM services

Despite the recent establishment of DFM, it has been able to provide many benefits to investors including:

- surveillance of operating activity through advanced information technology systems and qualified surveillance professionals, ensuring vet interest investors is maintained by avoiding manipulation in prices;
- transparency and disclosure of trading activity and company news assisting investors in making informed decisions;
- providing best security prices based on supply and demand;

- controlling and monitoring company disclosures to avoid rumours and manipulation;
- ease of liquidating securities by having a centralized system with all bids and offers based on priority of prices and order entry time;
- instant transfer of security ownership once a trade is executed;
- ensuring availability of securities before a trade is done to avoid any trade reversals;
- ensuring payment of broker to his/her client establishing a broker bank guarantee managed by DFM;
- standard maximum commission rates paid by investors to brokers;
- ease of trading through a centralized official location;
- facilitating the investment process by having all brokers in one securities exchange;
- qualified investor services employees, capable of providing investors with all required information while maintaining confidentiality.

DFM also offers various investor services that facilitate dealing with DFM including investor services desk, trading-floor services, CDS, supreme quote system, seminars and lecture presentations, website services, foreign investments.

Investor services desk

The desk addresses investor enquiries relating either to trading on DFM or to services provided by the bourse such as providing investor numbers, registering participants for the supreme quote system service, managing investor suggestions and complaints, and providing publications relating to DFM.

Trading-floor services

The trading floor has state-of-the-art facilities making trading at DFM a unique experience, particularly as investors can follow trading activity through electronic screens that display available bid and ask orders in the market. The floor is also equipped with computers that are connected to the electronic trading system that enables investors to follow trading in real time. Telephones are also available, enabling investors to give their orders to DFM brokers.

Investors' queries can be given to the floor coordinator for prompt responses. The floor also has offices for all DFM accredited brokers, as well as for the CDS department, to ensure the completion of investors' transactions in a highly efficient manner.

CDS

This department provides services in a quick, effective manner through the following functions:

- updating investors' information;
- issuing investor numbers;
- issuing account balances;
- producing confirmations;
- renewing and cancelling;
- DFM power of attorney;
- issuing proof of ownership letter;
- processing family, inheritance and judicial transfers;
- transferring securities between CDS and brokers and between brokers themselves;
- processing security transfers for trades conducted before DFM's establishment;
- receiving share certificates and depositing them electronically with DFM.

Supreme quote system

This service provides investors with instant DFM trading information through the use of a mobile telephone during the trading session. The service can alert an investor about the increase or decrease in a security's price through a pre-specified limit, and organize investor holding in a personal portfolio. Instant security prices can be provided through email as well as mobile phones.

Seminars and lecture presentations

DFM seeks to spread awareness and educate various society members about capital markets, DFM and the services it provides. This is done by organizing seminars and presentations either at DFM, or by visiting the interested parties requesting such seminars or presentations.

DFM website services

DFM provides, through its website (www.dfm.co.ae), several services aimed at providing as many investors as possible with valuable information that might influence security prices. This is to ensure that investors receive the same information at the same time, and to help them make informed decisions. Visitors of the site can follow DFM prices and trading activity, view trading charts for selected periods, view financial information of listed companies and its disclosures, and any related news. The site also contains DFM brochures and bulletins, DFM forms, requirement for listing the various types of securities, and broker licensing requirements.

Foreign investments at DFM

UAE companies' law allows non-UAE nationals to own up to 49 per cent of the capital of UAE public joint stock companies. However, many companies themselves forbid, according to the articles of incorporation, non-UAE nationals to own their shares.

Towards the end of 2000, Emaar Properties approved in its extraordinary general assembly a resolution allowing up to 20 per cent non-UAE ownership of its shares. Several companies have since been reconsidering allowing foreigners to participate in their companies, especially in the wake of the listing of the Emirates 2006 bond on DFM in July 2001. This was successfully open to non-UAE nationals. In addition, non-UAE investors can participate indirectly in the UAE capital markets by investing in mutual funds that are open to them and are managed by professional fund managers.

DFM achievements up to 2005

Listing securities

DFM has been striving to increase investment alternatives available to investors, and sources of financing available to companies through the UAE capital market. DFM was able to achieve the following during recent years:

- increase listed companies to 19 companies;
- list the first local bond in the UAE represented by Emirates EK-2006 bond in 2001. Another two bonds were listed later: Government of Dubai in 2003 and Shuaa Capital 2007 in 2004;

- list two more open-ended funds in 2004 to raise their total number to seven open-ended funds and one close-ended fund;
- issue the *Guide to Going Public and Listing on DFM*, which contains the details of converting a private company into a public joint stock company in the UAE through the initial public offering (IPO) process and then listing on DFM. The bourse has distributed hundreds of copies of this 60-page guide to interested parties.

Supervising trading and protecting participants

DFM has been working on enhancing its trading system to improve the level of transparency available. Features include:

- providing the Market Control Department with wide authorities to identify any suspicious transactions and notify DFM's Director General immediately for action;
- providing various priorities on the system, ensuring fairness in trading by specifying priorities by price and then time of entry;
- providing programmes linked to the trading system to enable the issuance of various trading reports for management to enable it to make appropriate decisions;
- possibility of displaying best 20 buy/sell orders for each listed security, and rank them by priority. This information is available on the computer monitors located on the DFM trading floor. Trading activity can also be monitored through the DFM website;
- managing the recording system in broker offices to ensure that they can be referred to in case of a dispute between an investor and a broker to protect their rights.

Improving disclosure and transparency

- DFM started issuing weekly, monthly and quarterly bulletins as well as an annual guide, in addition to the daily bulletins it has been issuing since its inception. These bulletins are intended to provide investors and other interested parties with information about DFM trading activity.
- DFM has been continuously developing its internet site to disseminate information affecting prices to all market participants simultaneously. Web pages covering company disclosures, results of annual general meetings and financial information have been added to the DFM site.

- The CDS division started mailing standard weekly activity reports to investors to present them with their activity at DFM. The bourse also produces customized reports.
- DFM launched the supreme quote system allowing investors to stay in touch with the market through the mobile phone, enabling them to get information on trading and prices from anywhere.

More efficient clearing and depository operations

- DFM's CDS division managed to exceed client expectations, including listed parties, investors and brokers, by increasing the efficiency in transfer of securities, issuing investor numbers, producing required information and reports and conducting corporate actions in record time.
- Corporate actions done by the division included share split, reverse share-split, bonus shares and cash dividends.
- DFM became the first Middle Eastern securities market to obtain ISO 9001:2000 certification.

Electronic link with Abu Dhabi Securities Market (ADSM)

DFM and ADSM established an electronic link during the summer of 2001 enabling DFM brokers to trade in ADSM-listed securities and vice versa.

Signing of depository agent agreement

DFM signed a depository agent agreement with HSBC Bank enabling international fund managers' participation in DFM-listed securities by meeting all statutory requirements of such managers through this agreement.

2.4

Dubai International Financial Centre: The Gateway to Regional Capital

DIFC

Introduction

The Dubai International Financial Centre (DIFC), the world's newest global financial hub, was declared open for business on 20 September 2004. On this day, a major step was taken towards completing the global financial system with the DIFC ideally located to bridge the gap left by the existing financial centres of London and New York in the West, and Hong Kong and Tokyo in the East.

20 September also saw the announcement of the first companies licensed to operate from within the centre. Swiss private bank, Julius Baer, was the first firm to receive a licence, followed by Standard Chartered and The GCC Energy Fund. Since launch, international firms of the calibre of Merrill Lynch, Mellon Global Investment, Barclays Capital, Lloyds TSB, HSBC, Credit Suisse, AON and Deutsche Bank have also applied or signalled their intent to apply for a licence. All of these institutions will receive benefits such as 0 per cent tax rate on income and profits, 100 per cent foreign ownership, no restrictions on foreign exchange or capital/profit repatriation, operational support and business continuity facilities.

The DIFC has been established by the government of Dubai to create a platform for further growth, progress and economic development in a region already investing an estimated US$1.8 trillion around the world. Focusing on the following main financial service sectors – banking services, capital markets, asset management and fund registration, reinsurance and insurance, Islamic finance, business processing operations and ancillary services – the vision of the DIFC is to become the universally recognized hub for institutional financial services in the region.

As with established international financial centres, at the heart of the overall DIFC concept is an independent regulator, the Dubai Financial Services Authority (DFSA). Staffed by experts with experience of working at leading regulatory agencies around the world, the DFSA is the independent regulatory and supervisory body that will grant licences and regulate the activities of financial institutions in the DIFC. It has been created using principle-based primary legislation modelled closely on that used in London and New York, and its regulatory regime will operate to standards that meet those of the world's major financial centres. Thus, this world-class regulatory framework, as well as the laws of the DIFC, will be familiar to the financial institutions and organizations that choose to locate in the DIFC and will provide legal certainty for their business operations.

A thriving exchange is at the heart of the world's major capital markets. This will also be the case at the DIFC following the establishment of the Dubai International Financial Exchange (DIFX). Launched on 26 September 2005, the DIFX will be a liquid and transparent electronic market trading shares, bonds and other securities, eventually including derivatives. It has been created to provide both investors and issuers with a larger and more liquid securities market than currently exists elsewhere in the region. The DIFX will not restrict investment to local investors, as some exchanges do, and will allow governments and companies globally to access regional investment opportunities. It is anticipated that companies outside the region will seek to have securities dual-listed on the exchange in order to benefit from the large pool of assets accessible in the region. The DIFX aims to facilitate anticipated privatizations in the region and enable initial public offerings (IPOs) by privately owned companies, giving impetus to the programme of deregulation and market liberalization throughout the region.

The physical infrastructure will also be a major factor in enticing international business to locate in the DIFC. So much more than just a financial district, the DIFC is planned to be a 'city within a city' that will comprise a unique integration of buildings and open spaces with over 65 per cent of the total site landscaped with specific green zones. It will ultimately provide over four million square feet of ultramodern office space, as well as residential and leisure areas that will include offices, serviced apartments, hotels, shops, restaurants, a museum, an art gallery and a performing arts centre.

Already beginning to transform Dubai's already breathtaking skyline, the DIFC site is characterized by the landmark 'Gate' building. Designed by leading international architects, Gensler, the Gate already houses the DIFC Authority, the DFSA and firms from the private sector. Credit Suisse was the first private-sector tenant of the Gate.

Guaranteeing the DIFC's success is its location. The cosmopolitan city of Dubai has a safe, secure environment that is economically, politically and socially stable; it also has superb infrastructure and a highly skilled, educated and multicultural workforce.

The DIFC initiative was first announced in early 2002 by the Crown Prince of Dubai, HH Sheikh Mohammed bin Rashid Al Maktoum, whose visionary leadership and efforts have already transformed the emirate. The success of Dubai's remarkable economic development can be attributed to a progressive and enlightened government whose vision and strategy for the country's economy includes the DIFC as a key component.

With such a sophisticated physical infrastructure, a visionary leadership and a stringent regulatory framework, the DIFC is poised to tap the largest emerging market for financial services with a region of 2.1 billion people and a combined economy worth US$1.8 trillion in terms of GDP, growing at an annual rate in excess of 5 per cent. It will also create a global centre for Islamic finance and create added reinsurance capacity in the region.

Now open for business, the DIFC is the complementary hub connecting the region to the 24hour/7 day-a-week global financial network. The world's newest international financial centre has become a reality and both the region and the world's financial community are set to benefit.

Operating structure of DIFC

DIFC Authority (DIFCA)

DIFCA is the body of the DIFC charged with developing overall strategy and providing direction and supervision to the Centre. Its responsibilities include the marketing of the DIFC and attracting licencees to operate in the Centre as well as the creation of laws and regulations to cover all aspects of non-financial activities that are not regulated by the DFSA, such as employment laws, company and commercial laws and real estate laws.

DIFCA officers include professionals drawn from leading banks, insurance companies, stock exchanges and other financial institutions who are entirely familiar with the exacting standards of service delivery expected of a world-class international financial centre.

DIFCA assists prospective licence applicants at every stage of the process – from providing research and assistance in the development of business plans, to the licence application process and obtaining visas and residency permits. Through its dedicated relationship managers, DIFCA will guide licence applicants through the entire process, offering a seamless, efficient and professional service.

Dubai International Financial Exchange (DIFX)

A wholly owned subsidiary of DIFCA, DIFX is led by a board of directors and senior staff with considerable experience in international and regional financial services. Regulation inside DIFX is provided by the DIFX Markets Authority, which operates independently of the commercial interests of the exchange. The DIFX trading platform will be provided by AtosEuronext and clearing and settlement services will be based on software provided by Tata Consultancy Services. DIFX is applying to DFSA for licences to operate an exchange and a clearing house.

DIFC Registrar of Companies (ROC)

A corporation sole administered by DIFCA, the DIFC Registrar is responsible for incorporating and registering all the companies that will operate within the DIFC, from multibillion-dollar financial institutions through to non-financial registrants seeking to establish a presence in the DIFC, as well as administering the companies law and regulations. By November 2005, over 100 companies were registered to operate from the DIFC.

Dubai Financial Services Authority (DFSA)

The DFSA is the integrated regulator of all financial and ancillary services undertaken in or from the DIFC. It is responsible for ensuring that the DIFC is one of the best-regulated financial centres in the world.

Created by statute and entirely independent of the DIFC, the DFSA is unique. While many regulatory bodies have been formed in response to financial crises, the DFSA has been established as a world-class regulator from the outset. Significantly, its framework is free from the confines and complexities that can develop when old systems are forced to fit new circumstances. The DFSA has been created specifically to suit the environment within which it operates.

Using a risk-based framework, the DFSA oversees the full range of financial and ancillary services in the DIFC. The DFSA is an Associate Member of the International Organization of Securities Commissions (IOSCO), the world's leading body of securities regulators.

DIFC Judicial Authority (DJA)

An autonomous body, the DJA is responsible for administering and enforcing civil and commercial laws at the DIFC. The DIFC Courts, including both trial and appellate courts, deal exclusively with all the cases and claims arising between DIFC-registered entities and out of the DIFC operations. The official language of the Courts is English. A Chief Justice was appointed in April 2005. He is responsible for the overall management of the administrative affairs of the DIFC Court and will preside over all appeals. Additionally, his role will encompass the establishment of circuits and divisions of the DIFC Courts, the appointment of its staff and its judicial officers, and the appointment of judicial officers as members of its tribunals.

Primary sectors of focus

The DIFC will focus on the following main financial service sectors: banking services, capital markets, asset management and fund registration, reinsurance and insurance, Islamic finance, business processing operations and ancillary services.

Banking services

Companies operating in the Middle East have, until now, had to rely on commercial or bank loans to finance development, which is both costly and inefficient. With Dubai's emergence as a major centre for international trade and with over 3,000 multinational and regional corporations located in its free zones requiring trade finance, the DIFC represents a significant opportunity to providers of trade finance.

Furthermore, there are more than 90 planned privatizations in the region and IPOs are increasingly used as mechanisms to raise capital. The DIFC will provide, through the DIFX, a more liquid, credibly regulated environment for such transactions to occur.

The DIFC will fast become the regional gateway for investment banks and other financial institutions who wish to establish underwriting, merger and acquisition (M&A) advisory, venture capital/private equity, foreign exchange, trade finance and capital markets operations in order to gain access to this large and relatively untapped market and take advantage of the growing opportunities in the region.

Capital markets: DIFX

The DIFX aims to become the premier international exchange in the Middle East, filling the gap between New York and London in the West, and Singapore and Hong Kong in the East. It is widely predicted to be the driving force for the further development of a robust capital market in the region, providing regional issuers with access to international and regional investors and being the conduit for international investors seeking exposure to the region.

The DIFX will be the main gateway to opportunities in the emerging markets of the Gulf Cooperation Council (GCC) states and the rest of the Middle East and North Africa, as well as South Africa, Turkey and the Indian subcontinent. For issuers from these areas it will offer increased market visibility, unprecedented access to regional and global capital and the ability to sustain fair valuation.

The DIFX intends to become the platform of choice in its region for a range of shares, bonds, funds, Islamic products, index products and eventually derivatives. Listings that the DIFX aims to attract include IPOs of shares, alternate listings for companies already quoted on other exchanges and fixed-income listings at both the corporate and sovereign levels.

Asset management and fund registration

Asset management firms and private banks have been very quick to realize the potential offered by the DIFC. Many top firms from all over the world have applied to become registered with the DIFC such as Mellon Global Investments, Franklin Templeton and Invesco. Attracted by a familiar regulatory regime, positive infrastructure and low-cost environment, fund managers will be able to offer a wide range of investment products such as mutual funds, exchange traded funds, open- and closed-ended investment companies, index funds, hedge funds, consultant wrap accounts and Islamic compliant funds. The Middle East has the highest concentration of high net worth and ultra high net worth individuals in the world.

Reinsurance

Insurance levels in the region have been well below those seen in other parts of the world. This reflects a combination of factors including a general lack of insurance awareness, social and religious inhibitions, great reliance on social welfare systems and low disposable incomes that have all resulted in depressed demand for insurance products. However, trends for this sector have changed in recent years, brought about by the recent economic development, industrialization and rapid growth of trade in the region. The huge infrastructural spending on projects within the energy, water, transportation and petrochemicals sectors, as well as the privatization of state utilities and other assets, have all resulted in greater demand for insurance and reinsurance coverage.

Separately, the region has experienced a changing attitude towards risk in recent years, especially with the dramatic growth of Islamic finance and with the introduction of Islamic-compliant insurance products such as Takaful – a market expected to grow at nearly 20 per cent per annum, making it one of the fastest expanding financial industries in the world. It is highly likely that the insurance industry will witness the highest percentage of growth compared with any other financial industry in the region.

The DIFC will promote the insurance and reinsurance industry in the region by creating a thriving centre comprising various components of the insurance industry from insurers, reinsurers and brokers to service, educational and training providers.

The DIFC also seeks to raise the profile of the regional insurance industry and create better awareness of insurance products that are not widely known or available in the region. It will also act as the link between the regional insurance market and international insurance associations and initiate and sponsor insurance-related research and publications. Additionally, it will provide an investment channel for local insurers and reinsurers to invest in the international market.

Islamic finance

The DIFC will emerge as the regional hub for Islamic banking and finance serving large Islamic communities around the region. The centre offers an opportunity for both Islamic and non-Islamic banks looking to offer Shariah-compliant financial products to develop a centre of excellence and understanding for the development of this vastly ambitious industry.

In drawing up its legal and regulatory framework governing Islamic banks and financial institutions, the DIFC has sought input and consulted with leading scholars, academics and international organizations on the subject. This has resulted in a framework that is transparent, supportive of an Islamic financial system and in line with international best practices governing finance.

The future growth and development of the Islamic banking and finance industry largely depends on the degree of innovation introduced in the market. The DIFC aims to become the centre for product development to meet the funding requirements and rapidly increasing demand and sophistication of investors. Through its cooperation with leading Islamic scholars, academics and banking institutions in the region, the DIFC will fuel the development and structuring of more complex, liquid and long-term, Islamic-denominated products that satisfy the broad needs of both investors and issuers.

The DIFC will also boost training and research within Islamic finance and increase awareness and understanding of Islamic finance both within the region and in the West. To this end, the DIFC will sponsor seminars, lectures and forums on topics relevant to Islamic finance.

Business processing operations

The growth of back-office operations has been a permanent feature of the financial services industry in recent years. With its world-class IT infrastructure and ready access to the region's large pool of educated and skilled professionals, Dubai is well placed to become the location of choice of the global back-office operations of banks and other financial institutions. The DIFC offers a very attractive proposition as a location for support activities.

Ancillary services

The financial institutions operating from the DIFC will find the same services and quality of support as in any other major financial centre. The DIFC will attract top law firms, accountancy practices, recruitment consultancies and other ancillary services, themselves benefiting from zero tax, a state of the art infrastructure and safe and secure environment.

2.5

The National Bank of Dubai

The National Bank of Dubai

Founded in 1963, the National Bank of Dubai (NBD) is the oldest locally incorporated bank in the southern Gulf. From its imposing new headquarters, depicting a ship in full sail, it operates 40 branches in the UAE plus one branch in London and a representative office in Tehran.

Business activities

Corporate banking

A key division of NBD, corporate banking offers a comprehensive suite of products and services that support the requirements of its corporate clientele and include a full range of trade finance, treasury, lending and deposit-taking services, which are offered to all UAE-based customers. NBD works with a broad range of transportation, tourism and government client segments, serving as a leader in providing professional and responsive relationship banking to all of its customers.

Treasury products and services

NBD enjoys a pre-eminent position in the dirham money market, being an active market maker. The bank is also active on the foreign exchange markets. Its dealers actively track the global markets and provide advice to customers on exchange markets and interest-rate outlook.

'The Private Office': NBD private banking services

The Private Office of NBD has been established with the commitment to preserve and protect the personal wealth of its customers, offering highly responsive tailored solutions emphasizing a total relationship management approach. The primary objective of 'The Private Office' is to provide its customers with world-class solutions for three of their most important requirements: wealth preservation and growth, investment management and succession and estate planning.

Through the bank's external alliances with world-class financial institutions, clients can easily access a menu of varied solutions, depending on their current and future investment schemes and profiles, with an active focus on risk management and yield enhancement. UK Commercial Real Estate Investment Service is offered through NBD London as a distinct service to assist in making the most informed investment choices in a complex market. NBD London has selected and created a panel of external specialists, familiar with Middle Eastern investors' needs, to assist in the acquisition, finance and ownership of commercial real estate investments in London. National Bank of Dubai Trust Company (Jersey) Ltd has been formed with support from, and consultation with, a world-class financial institution. Through the trust company, customers are provided with access to experts in the field of offshore trusts and structures in well-established, politically stable and reliable jurisdictions including the Caribbean, Europe and Asia. Moreover, The Private Office launched the NBD Gulf Balanced Fund, the bank's first in-house managed fund. The primary objective of the Fund is to seek capital growth by investing in a portfolio of Gulf Cooperation Council (GCC) and regional equities, bonds and other securities issued by GCC governments and corporations. The Fund has been listed on the Dubai Financial Market.

The objective of The Private Office is to work in close partnership with customers as individuals and family businesses on the basis of absolute confidentiality, trust, honesty and integrity. In order to ensure the growth and protection of their wealth from generation to generation, individual and unique requirements need careful consultation and consideration.

Retail banking and card services

NBD has a long history of banking excellence. Its retail service philosophy combines the Arab tradition of hospitality and care with the efficiency and precision of modern technology. The bank's mission is to establish itself as the 'preferred neighbourhood bank', providing easily accessible and dependable banking support to people across the emirates.

Complementing its branch network are its off-site ATMs. NBD pioneered the first stand-alone ATM in the UAE in 1986 and today customers can withdraw cash and pay utility bills through a network of more than 115 ATMs, as well as utilize point of sale terminals installed at a large number of hotels and stores. The bank's automated banking services, which comprise an internet service (NBD Online), a telebanking facility (NBD Telebank) and an SMS-based service (NBD Mobile), are a result of its efforts to provide easy accessibility and ensure banking convenience for its customers.

Its business portfolio includes exclusive service-based products for special customer segments, namely the Abeer, a banking service exclusively designed for women, and the Ajial Savings account, aimed at young people aged 18–25 years. With regard to asset-based products, the bank offers a suite of choices including secured facilities, personal loans and auto loans. NBD's conventional offering of deposit products has been further augmented by the introduction of retail investment products. The bank also recently launched Suhail Priority Banking Services, a premier banking service offering customers personalized relationship management and a host of exclusive products and services.

In addition to a range of credit benefits, the bank's card portfolio includes Visa Premier and Classic as well Platinum, Gold and Standard MasterCard credit cards.

Investing in technology

NBD has been at the forefront of identifying and investing in new banking technology to support its operations and to respond to the needs of the community services. The bank, together with other UAE banking institutions, played a leading role in introducing SWIFT, the international telecommunications system for sending and receiving financial data. It was among the first banks to join the UAE Switch linking the ATMs of major UAE banks. The bank launched its website in June 1998.

Investing in people

NBD's prominence in the business community means it has a special role to play in helping to develop the country. While the bank employs more than 1,100 people drawn from 29 countries, it is proud that more than 32 per cent of its workforce are UAE nationals.

NBD has an ongoing commitment to providing training and development opportunities, to enable UAE nationals to build banking careers and help the development of the UAE. Specially designed and developed training programmes underpin the bank's commitment to 'emiratization' and preservation of its traditional values of quality and service. NBD received the Dubai Human Development Award for 2002 in the financial sector and the Human Recources Development Award in the banking sector for the year 2003, in recognition of its efforts in the field of emiratization.

Awards received

Over the years NBD has received a number of awards proving the bank's high-quality performance. In February 2004, it was named Best Foreign Exchange Bank in the UAE by the magazine, *Global Finance*. The success story continued throughout the year: in March the bank was ranked the fourth best bank and the first local bank in the UAE for private banking services in a worldwide survey conducted by *EuroMoney*. In May, for the second consecutive year, it was chosen as the Best Bank in the UAE by *Global Finance*. And for the seventh time, NBD received the Quality Recognition Award from JP Morgan Chase Bank in recognition of the high level of accuracy in money-transfering procedures.

2.6

Hedge-Fund Investing in the Gulf

Robert A Jaeger, Vice Chairman and Chief Investment Officer, EACM Advisors LLC

Introduction

The hedge fund business is booming, and the Gulf region is an important part of that growth.* Although most hedge funds are located outside the Gulf region (mainly in the USA and Europe), many Gulf investment funds have become important sources of capital for hedge funds. Gulf investors either invest in hedge funds directly or they use 'funds of funds', which are broadly diversified portfolios that invest in multiple underlying hedge funds, often as many as 30 or more. Moreover, the Gulf region is poised to become an important source of services for hedge funds. The founding of the Dubai International Financial Centre (DIFC) means that Dubai may eventually rival Bermuda, the Cayman Islands and Dublin as a major offshore financial centre.

Although the hedge fund business has been growing steadily for many years, the growth accelerated after the global bull market unraveled in the early part of 2000. According to commonly accepted estimates, there are now almost 10,000 hedge funds managing aggregate assets of almost US$1 trillion. The universe of hedge funds includes a small number of multibillion-dollar funds, as well as a large number of very small funds, with assets of less than US$25 million. Much of the money in hedge funds is funneled through funds of funds, of which there are nearly a thousand.

* For the purposes of this article, the Gulf region is, essentially, the six countries of the Gulf Cooperation Council (GCC): Saudi Arabia, Kuwait, Bahrain, Qatar, the United Arab Emirates and Oman.

What are hedge funds, and why are they so popular? Hedge funds share four common characteristics that separate them from traditional investment funds:

- absolute return objective;
- strategy flexibility;
- exclusivity;
- performance fees.

Absolute return objective

Hedge funds try to earn a positive investment return, independent of market conditions. This return objective is often expressed as a premium over LIBOR (or some other proxy for the risk-free rate of return). Conservative hedge funds will aim for a premium of 2 per cent or 3 per cent, while more aggressive funds will aim for a premium of 10 per cent or more. In any case, the return objective is always a positive number, whereas traditional investment funds generally try to beat market-related benchmarks that have the potential to be negative. If a US-oriented equity manager loses 18 per cent when the Standard & Poor's 500 is down 20 per cent, the manager will feel proud even though his clients have lost money. In the world of hedge funds, positive returns are the name of the game.

Strategy flexibility

Traditional money managers take long positions only. They buy what looks attractive to them, and may hold cash if opportunities dry up. Hedge funds can take long or short positions, and they can use options, futures or other derivatives. They can also use leverage, which not only increases the return potential, but also increases the risk profile of the portfolio. The ability to take short positions is essential to achieving the absolute return objective: the only way to make money in a down market is through short positions or related strategies, such as owning puts.

Exclusivity

Many traditional money managers build retail-oriented businesses organized around a large number of small clients. Hedge funds organize themselves around a smaller number of large and more sophisticated clients. In most countries hedge funds are not allowed to market themselves to the general public. This gives them a certain amount of social cachet: investing in the fund is like belonging to an exclusive club. Adding to the cachet is the fact that the hedge-fund manager may well be an investment 'star' (or alleged star, or star for the moment) who has a very large amount of his or her own money invested in the fund. (The exclusivity feature is gradually changing as hedge-fund managers exploit legal structures that enable them to sell their services to a broader audience. Still, a key element of the sales pitch is that the smaller investor now has access to investment talent once available only to a select group.)

Performance fees

Traditional money managers charge asset-based fees. They grow rich by raising large amounts of assets. Hedge-fund managers charge a combination of asset-based and performance-based fees. A typical fee would be 1 per cent of the assets plus 20 per cent of the return. In a good year, the performance fee will be larger than the asset-based fee. In theory, the incentive arrangement means that the hedge-fund manager should concentrate on *managing* assets (generating good performance) rather than on *gathering* assets (growing his asset base). However, the incentive arrangement also gives the manager a 'free call' on the fund's performance, which may create an incentive to take extra risk. This risk is, however, mitigated by the fact that most hedge-fund managers are 'long term greedy' – they want to own a share of a longer-term stream of performance and are not merely to looking for a short term 'pop' in performance.

Differences in hedge funds

For the serious hedge-fund investor, the differences among hedge funds are more important than the similarities. The world of hedge funds is not a homogeneous, monolithic universe; it is tremendously varied, embracing many different strategies and many different risk levels. The main strategies are:

- *Relative value investing*. Relative value investors construct hedged portfolios emphasizing security selection within a market while minimizing net directional exposure to that market. Examples include market neutral equity, convertible hedging and fixed income arbitrage.

- *Event-driven investing.* Event-driven investors focus on mergers, acquisitions, financial reorganizations (including bankruptcies) and other corporate events. Although event-driven investors focus on very 'situation-specific' investments, they are usually long-biased.
- *Equity hedge funds.* Equity hedge funds are stock pickers ('micro investors') who use leverage and short selling techniques; they may be net-long, net-short, or net-neutral as market circumstances change. Within the world of equity hedge funds there are style differences very similar to the traditional equity style differences: there are growth managers and value managers, industry specialists, regional specialists and so forth. The large category of equity hedge funds includes the much smaller category of *short sellers,* who are consistently net-short equities. As their risk/return profile is very different from that of the more typical equity hedge fund, it is useful to consider them a separate group.
- *Global asset allocators.* Global asset allocators are 'macro investors' who take long or short positions in equity indices, interest rates, currencies and physical commodities. Some managers use highly quantitative technical trading systems, others follow a more discretionary approach that uses fundamental input. This category includes commodity trading advisors (CTAs).

The performance of hedge-fund strategies

The historical performance of the various hedge-fund strategies has been very attractive (Figure 2.6.1[†]). The left-hand chart in Figure 2.6.1 shows return versus standard deviation. (Standard deviation, which measures the variability of return, is an imperfect, but widely used, proxy for risk.) Notice that many hedge-fund strategies lie above many of the traditional market benchmarks: they have delivered higher return for the same risk, or they have delivered the same return with lower risk.

The right-hand chart shows performance in down markets: how do hedge funds perform when the traditional markets are negative? Here we use the Standard & Poor's 500 as the reference market. During this time period, US equities posted a negative return in 38 per cent of the months, with an average monthly loss of 4 per cent. For the hedge-fund strategies, there are two questions: (1) How often do they make money in down markets? and (2) What is their average return in down

† These charts are based on the performance of the EACM100® Index of Hedge Funds, which was created in 1995 and has been published monthly since January 1996.

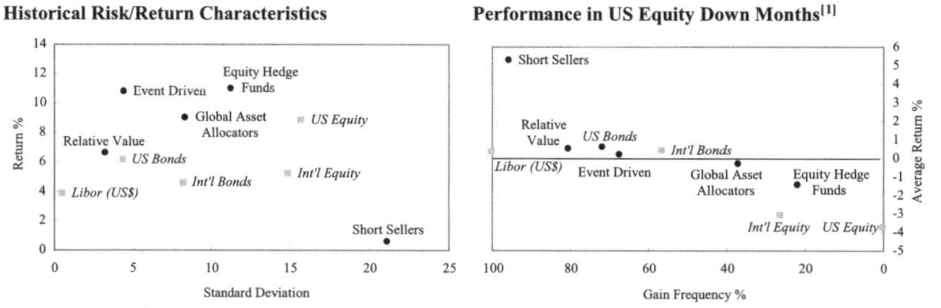

[1] US Equity represented by the S&P 500 Index. For the period shown, the S&P 500 was down 39.0% of the time, with an average monthly loss of 3.76%.

Analysis based on statistical measures calculated from monthly total returns for the period January 1996 through October 2005. Source: Standard & Poor's 500, MSCI EAFE $, Lehman Bros Govt/Credit Index, Citigroup World Govt Bond ex US Index ($), Merrill Lynch 90 Day T-Bills and EACM100® Index. Performance results for the various hedge fund strategies are derived from strategy component returns for the EACM100® Index Onshore Funds (January 1990 – December 2003) and EACM100® Index – Offshore Funds (January 2004 – October 2005). See www.eacm.com for more information regarding the EACM100® Index.

Figure 2.6.1. Historical performance of hedge fund strategies

markets? As you can see, most hedge-fund strategies have done a good job of preserving capital in down markets.

Hedge funds and the Gulf

Given the potential for hedge funds to deliver a very attractive combination of return and risk, it is not surprising that substantial Gulf assets have flowed into this area. In effect, the use of hedge funds represents the second stage of economic diversification. The first stage was the creation of global securities portfolios to invest the wealth created by massive energy resources. This move creates a natural hedge: high oil prices are good for the local economies but potentially harmful to the global securities portfolio; low oil prices have the opposite effect. But the global securities portfolio is a long-only portfolio whose performance is determined ultimately by the performance of the underlying markets. The second stage of diversification is to create a portion of the securities portfolio whose return is less dependent on the performance of the underlying markets. That is exactly the role that hedge funds are designed to play.

A small number of large Gulf investment funds have become very active in investing directly in hedge funds. They have built up internal investment staffs with the specialized expertise required to conduct effective due diligence in a very complicated area. They rely on that expertise to build diversified portfolios using multiple strategies and multiple managers. Diversification is the key to success. Different strategies march to different drummers, and manager-specific risk is much higher in the hedge-fund world than in the traditional world. The success of a hedge fund is critically dependent on the investment judgement of one or two key people, and when things go wrong in the hedge-fund world, they can go very wrong indeed. The ultimate disasters are frauds (eg misrepresenting performance or stealing from investors) and 'blow-ups' (dramatic losses in which investment errors combine with high leverage to produce lethal results). The most famous blow-up was the case of Long-Term Capital Management, which was managed by one of the most illustrious investment teams ever assembled. Despite their combined brainpower, their fund came apart in the latter part of 1998 as the global financial system was shaken by Russia's debt default and currency devaluation.

For those investors who do not have the internal resources to master the complexities of hedge-fund investing, the natural solution is a fund of funds – a diversified portfolio managed by a firm with specialized expertise in hedge-fund investing. The fund-of-funds manager adds a second layer of fees, but many investors find that the extra fees are justified by access to professional management and broad diversification. Some funds of funds are managed by independent investment boutiques, others are managed by large financial institutions (commercial banks and investment banks) or subsidiaries of such institutions. Most fund-of-funds managers are located outside the Gulf region, mainly in the USA and Europe; however, some Gulf institutions have developed an internal fund-of-funds capability of their own, and other Gulf institutions have developed alliances and partnerships with non-Gulf specialists.

The hedge funds (and funds of funds) that are available in the Gulf are offshore funds domiciled in Bermuda, the Cayman Islands, or some other offshore financial centre. That means that various 'back-office functions' (custody, fund administration and so forth) are located offshore. In addition, the offshore country provides the regulatory regime that determines how the fund is governed. All these functions are totally separate from the investment management function, which is more likely to be located in the USA, Europe or elsewhere.

The creation of the DIFC adds a new competitor to the list. As plans now stand, the DIFC is likely to offer two crucial benefits to the hedge-fund community. First, the DIFC will strive to become an important legal domicile for offshore funds – a centre for various fund administrative services. Although Dubai-based funds would have a special appeal for Gulf-based investors, the DIFC's ultimate ambition is to create a 'brand' that would be appealing to hedge-fund investors all over the world.

Second, the ambitions of the DIFC are not confined to fund administration. The DIFC plans to create new financial markets for the trading of stocks, bonds and derivative instruments. As things now stand, many of the Gulf stock exchanges are subject to capital controls that can make it difficult, or impossible, for non-Gulf investors to invest in

Gulf companies. The DIFC plans to operate under rules that would make it easier for non-Gulf capital to flow into Gulf companies. And it is safe to assume that a noticeable portion of that capital will be managed by hedge funds. If everything works according to plan, the DIFC will provide the classic 'matchmaking' function of an open capital market. Hedge funds will uncover a potentially important new set of investment opportunities, and Gulf-based companies will gain access to a potentially important new source of capital.

2.7

The Insurance Environment

Paul W Holmes, Country Manager, UAE, AXA Insurance (Gulf) BSC

Introduction

The UAE offers a highly diverse trading environment. Traditionally it was dominated by the huge petrochemical investments in Abu Dhabi, a world-leading aluminium producer in Dubai and a vibrant re-export trade – a key ingredient behind Dubai's success in recent years. There is now a greater emphasis on diversification of the economy, with rapid development of the tourism, manufacturing, real-estate and financial sectors, amongst others. The insurance industry continues to keep pace with the development of the economy and, as *laissez-faire* policies are followed in order to keep pace with World Trade Organization (WTO) initiatives and requirements and the eco-nomy continues to flourish, it is expected to play an even greater role.

The total insurance market premium for 2005 is estimated to be almost US$1.6 billion in an industry employing over 3,400 persons. Of this, an estimated US$300 million relates to 'life business' with the remaining share falling into the 'general business' category. UAE is the third largest insurance market in the Middle East which, considering its relatively small population, reflects its economic expansion and diversification of the economy over recent years.

There are 47 insurers in the UAE, many of which are foreign companies licensed to trade in the country. The industry is regulated by the Ministry of Economy and Planning in accordance with various federal laws and ministerial decrees issued over the past 25 years. The Ministry of Economy and Planning governs the industry in such matters as licensing, solvency margins, capitalization, financial reporting, mandatory covers and other compliance and regulatory matters. The Emirates Insurance Association (EIA) is affiliated to the

Ministry of Economy and Planning and provides a conduit for official representation and development of the industry. Various technical committees of industry representatives have been formed by the EIA in order to advise on industry issues.

The traditional distribution channels of insurance companies (direct and broker) exist, with broker representation dominating the market. The emirate of Dubai has probably seen a greater level of innovation in recent years including the development of customer-centric call centres. Curiously, the UAE has not developed a sophisticated banc-assurance distribution channel, which is partly due to restrictions imposed by the industry regulator. However, it is anticipated that this will change in the near future as the sophistication of the financial sector is developing at a significant rate and regulatory disciplines will need to match this development.

Takaful insurance companies and the provision of Takaful products is an area receiving significant attention within the Middle East – the UAE is no exception. Takaful is perceived as cooperative insurance and is often compared to the principles to which mutual companies adhere, whereby it is accepted under Islamic law. The development of such propositions are, of course, very appealing to Muslim communities and are therefore likely to become increasingly important in the Middle East over the coming years.

As part of the vision for growth, progress and economic development, HH Sheikh Mohammed bin Rashid Al Maktoum and the government of Dubai have created the Dubai International Finance Centre (DIFC). This is an onshore capital market designated as a financial free zone and designed to create a unique financial services cluster economy for wealth creation initiatives. Reinsurance is one of the six primary sectors within DIFC and is likely to attract many new players to participate in creating an extremely dynamic insurance industry in the region.

With 47 insurers, 150 brokers and an estimated premium income of US$1.6 billion, the UAE insurance industry is chronically overcrowded and one would predict consolidation for both insurers and intermediaries given normal market dynamics. Although we have seen some merger activity in recent years (the most recent in 2005 between AXA and Norwich Union), these have largely been driven by exogenous factors rather than a result of chronic overcapacity. However, recent developments permitting entry by foreign insurance companies and the establishment of a financial free zone would suggest that many of the local insurers will need to consider consolidation and/or regional expansion into other markets in the coming years, if they are to survive in an even more dynamic and competitive industry.

Corporate insurances

Governmental and quasi-governmental business in Abu Dhabi is often shared between six national companies operating from the emirate, and other insurers rarely have the opportunity of writing these risks. This is much the same for contract business in Abu Dhabi and although the price is often competitive, the servicing levels may not meet expectations if compared with European counterparts. Other emirates do not see such a significant restriction in placement of such risks. The *laissez-faire* environment that has developed in the emirate of Dubai has created an extremely dynamic and competitive market place, thus providing corporate customers with better insurance solutions at extremely competitive prices.

Property business

Most private businesses in the UAE are insured. Property cover that is available ranges from a 'restricted perils' policy, which would cover such risks as fire and explosion, to a 'property all risks' policy, which extends to provide for a variety of contingencies including accidental damage. Many of the wordings utilized are based on traditional UK market wordings and accepted as the norm within the insurance industry. Properties of very high value or of specialist nature are often reinsured in Europe as the local market may not have the capacity or expertise to underwrite these. This is common to most markets.

The UAE has been fortunate over recent years and has not suffered many significant property losses. The natural hazards (such as storms and earthquakes) have proven to be infrequent and major losses due to fire have been quite rare. As a result, we have seen tremendous competition for this type of business, which has led to significant reductions in premium levels – often below economic levels – that may not be sustainable in the long term. A recent fire in 2005 completely destroyed a large shopping centre and is likely to prove to be the single largest fire loss ever seen in the UAE. A number of insurers were involved in the claim and this may well have an impact on pricing and assessment of large fire exposures in the future.

The UAE, particularly Dubai, is well known for its logistics businesses and a corollary of this is the development of extensive warehousing, often with significant values at risk. Insurers are quite cautious in underwriting such risks due to the exposure at any one location. The quality insurers will usually provide a risk survey accompanied with risk management advice to help reduce the risk exposure.

Recent warehouse fires have, at least for the short term, forced insurers to exercise a higher degree of caution in accepting such risks. In fact, curiously, civil defence authorities have subsequently suggested that insurance companies should be responsible for ensuring that risks comply with the minimum safety standards prescribed by the authorities before accepting the risk, and have suggested legislation along these lines to come into play in the near future. Although the more service-oriented insurers are likely to specifically advise on risk management, the imposition of minimum safety and construction standards clearly rests with the local or federal authorities. Perhaps, in the future, we will see some effective collaboration to achieve a desirable outcome benefiting all.

Business interruption (also known as 'consequential loss') insurance, which covers loss of profits following an insured property loss such as a fire or storm, is usually advocated as an important cover. However, this cover is not frequently taken up in the UAE, a decision that is, of course, always regretted following a significant loss in a fire, for example. There are various derivatives of this cover designed to cater for specific needs (eg advanced loss of profits/increased cost of working) but they are not often utilized due to lack of understanding/explanation or sometimes preoccupation with price only.

Liability

The UAE has fewer liability claims compared with the far more litigious cultures of Europe, the USA or Canada. Also, the size of awards is generally not very significant. This could change in the future as it is recognized that awards for death and disablement following negligence are relatively low for a developing economy where a minimum standard of living is now expected. This is witnessed by a government decree in 2004 increasing the awards of *Diya* or 'blood money' to some US$55,000 per person from US$41,000 in the event of death due to negligence. However, one is unlikely to see the kind of awards prevalent in the West becoming the norm.

Employer's liability and public liability insurances are compulsory for companies operating in the free zones such as Jebel Ali. Dubai's government's recent initiative to set up a new industrial city and increasing efforts to promote and develop free zones is expected to attract more multinational manufacturing companies thereby giving a boost to both public and products liability insurances. Even though local awards can be much lower than those found in Western society, it is of course prudent to cover these liabilities in any event, particularly when exporting products or services overseas or dealing with companies or individuals who may be able to take legal action in other territories.

There is an increasing trend to substitute workmen's compensation cover by obtaining group life and personal accident insurance and a simple top-up employer's liability policy covering only occupational sicknesses as required by Sharia law. This is generally more cost effective and extends the coverage by providing death due to any cause, rather than just accidental death.

Construction/engineering insurance

Over the past few years there has been tremendous growth in the UAE construction sector. Iconic projects such as the Palm, World, Burj Dubai and Dubai Waterfront have placed the UAE firmly on the world map as a leader in exciting and cutting-edge construction projects. Dubai's light rail project is also a major development, which could present a different range of risks associated with construction and maintenance of railways – a concept new to the UAE.

The level of expertise, specialization and diversity within the construction industry in the UAE has significantly increased over recent years in line with demand. Other support functions have expanded to keep pace with the construction boom, including expertise of construction and engineering insurance. Covers and policy wording have been extended to provide very wide coverage while premium levels are some of the lowest anywhere in the world. Some of the international insurers believe the premium levels are uneconomically low considering the extended policy coverage and have declined to participate in some risks.

The project finance, and consequently some of the insurance covers, for very large and complex projects are often negotiated in the international arena, usually Europe, prior to local participation. Such projects require a high level of capacity and specialization that may not be available in the local insurance market; thus more realistic and sustainable premium terms are usually obtained.

Associated professionals such as engineers and architects also require insurance covers for such risks as professional negligence, defective design and the like. These are available locally but underwriting expertise is usually provided by the reinsurance companies specializing in these areas.

Latent defect has also become a common request by developers. The industry is seeing a movement to a 10-year discovery period that is currently treated very cautiously by the insurance market, given the relatively recent but very significant construction boom in the UAE.

Medical

Medical insurance has grown rapidly in the UAE in recent years and this trend is likely to continue for some years to come as the government's intention to shift the burden of cost from the public to the private sectors is realized. Currently, unless one is able to show evidence of private medical insurance with a locally registered insurer, the government charges each expatriate approximately US$82 for a health card when a work permit is issued. The health card entitles the holder to medical services for a nominal fee at government-owned hospitals. However, the increasing trend is for employers to provide private health insurance for their employees.

The provision of quality private healthcare has developed rapidly in recent years and the corresponding supply of insurance has developed alongside it. Most registered insurance companies provide group medical insurance schemes, some also provide a facility for individuals. The types of products and services provided are diverse, ranging from basic low-cost reimbursement schemes to sophisticated international direct billing schemes. Familiar names such as BUPA and PPP provide international network coverage and the provision of worldwide portability of cover for individuals.

We are likely to see the implementation of a compulsory health insurance law in 2006 that will require all employers to provide a minimum level of health insurance for their expatriate employees, thus reducing the burden on the public sector but ensuring that all individuals have the ability to seek medical treatment.

Marine cargo

The ports and airports of the UAE have fast become major international centres for cargoes being sent around the Gulf Cooperation Council (GCC) countries and the rest of the world. The many free zones, industrial cities, the favourable economic environment and general development have fuelled a surge in trading, manufacturing, distribution and transportation logistics for all kinds of goods. All this presents significant opportunities and challenges to the marine insurance underwriter. Risks vary from imports from the Far East, exports/re-exports to Iran (one of Dubai's key re-export markets), Africa, Caspian Sea ports, the former CIS or even further afield. Notwithstanding the journey or hazards, businesspersons are able to obtain coverage at competitive prices, even for shipments by dhow (a traditional Arabic vessel).

The increasing tendency for the UAE to attract international business and its growing position on the world financial stage have encouraged international traders to base themselves within the country. Risks now being presented to local underwriters do not even touch the Middle East, let alone the UAE.

Marine covers provided by insurers in the UAE mirror international requirements, while the service delivery is dependent upon the provider. Service by insurers at the top end of the market is excellent with in-depth understanding of the logistics chain, risk management advice and electronic policy issuing facilities. Premiums are extremely competitive.

Iraqi trade is a growing sector for the UAE and, once greater stability is restored, will be a major development area for traders. Most insurers are wary and are still carefully monitoring the situation in Iraq, however insurers willing to insure such cargoes find no shortage in demand for such cover. The few insurers willing to take the risk offer a very limited cover and only on a case-by-case basis. This is expected to continue unless there is a significant improvement in the security situation.

With development of new port and airport infrastructures and the growing logistics network currently being built in the UAE, we see even further growth in the transportation of cargoes for many years to come.

Group life

Group life covers are usually based on the traditional term assurance annual contracts and are often purchased in association with group personal accident covers. 'Employee benefits' are becoming an increasingly important factor in retaining and recruiting staff in the UAE and one is now seeing the introduction of group pension provision. As employers provide a mandatory leaving indemnity to their staff, some of the more sophisticated products are now able to utilize this indemnity in the form of pension provision whereby employee and/or employer are able to provide further contributions. This is a recent development but is likely to become an important growth area in the future as the labour market becomes more deregulated and employers compete to retain/recruit good-quality employees.

Personal insurance

Motor

Motor insurance is mandatory in the UAE, and registration or renewal thereof is subject to provision of a certificate of insurance for a 13-month period. The vehicle is then registered for 12 months and the 13th month is given as a grace period to reregister the vehicle for the following year. The 13-months insurance requirement is intended to reduce the number of uninsured vehicles on the roads.

Over 70 per cent of cars are insured comprehensively making it the largest class of insurance business in the UAE. There is a mandatory minimum level of cover, which provides for 'third party' liabilities; this is called the 'unified policy'. However, reputable insurers will provide covers wider than the minimum, with some providing cover and service levels to UK standards with such innovations as provision of a hire car, roadside assistance and the like. It is important to look for the provision of these benefits as well as checking out the claims philosophies, for example: will repairs be carried out at the insurer's appointed garage or the agency garage, and does the insurance company guarantee repairs?

Although the road infrastructure is excellent and driving standards are better in the UAE than in many Arab countries, much higher traffic volumes have led to dramatic increases in claims frequencies and a corresponding deterioration in insurers' motor portfolio in recent years. This has been exacerbated by increasing repair costs as well as the undercutting of rates in a fiercely competitive insurance market.

On the liability side, death claims are settled by way of a minimum payment of US$54,300 to the victim's family in terms of the governing Sharia law; this is referred to as *Diya* ('blood money'). If there is disablement then a medical committee will report to the court, which will then decide the award. Serious injury cases frequently go to the civil court where awards above the *Diya* are likely; there have been numerous claims over US$500,000 when permanent disablement is involved.

Home

Most Western expatriates insure their household possessions and, although crime is not very prominent, it is on the increase. Individuals will, in any case, be protected against virtually any eventuality as occasional winter storms create significant numbers of water damage claims.

There is a limited provision of good-quality packaged products. However, the few available do measure up to those available in the UK or Europe with the provision for covers such as buildings, contents, personal effects and valuables as well as other 'add-on' covers such as personal liability.

Dubai was the first emirate of the UAE to offer expatriates the facility to purchase properties on a freehold basis. The resulting boom in the homebuilding and property market has obviously had a beneficial effect on home-loan business for banks and, correspondingly, increased demand for home buildings insurance, often administered as a scheme between the insurance company and the lending institution.

Other personal lines products

Other traditional personal lines products such as travel, personal accident and medical insurance are available; some of the more sophisticated insurers provide similar products to those found in the UK or Europe.

Call centres, bancassurance, life and investment products

Although still a relatively new concept in the UAE, insurance call centres have gained momentum over the last few years. There are a number of recently established insurance call centres where one can undertake the entire business transaction over the phone in a quick and efficient manner. These call centres are evolving and will soon be providing a full service proposition for personal lines customers, including claims assistance.

The holistic financial services approach of selling insurance products via retail banks, commonly known in Europe as 'bancassurance', has not been developed in a sophisticated and comprehensive manner in the UAE to date. Current legislation has precluded widespread development of bancassurance partnerships, although it is possible via application to both the insurance and banking regulators to gain an exemption to develop this distribution channel. A number of banks have developed specific product schemes such as motor and home to assist in the development of their business.

Life and investment ('wealth management') products are limited in the UAE and there are only a handful of registered international insurers providing products in this area. Banks are also developing quickly in this area and most banks are now able to offer investment products to their customers that are, in fact, regulated by the Central Bank. Many of the national insurers have been studying this market and some have now developed their own products to compete with the limited number of international plans available. We are likely to see regulation helping to develop this sector in the future.

Takaful companies are developing compliant products to compete with the traditional 'Western' orientated products. These are receiving increasing interest from the insuring public as well as becoming attractive to the Islamic banking and finance institutions in the UAE.

Conclusion

The UAE is a colourful and interesting insurance market, which continues to experience rapid development. The industry is likely to continue to see greater innovation in products and services in the future as it expands in a more flexible but well governed environment.

Part Three

Prospective Sectors for Investment

Sectoral Investment Opportunities in Dubai

3.1

Dubai: Industrial Sectors

Data Management and Business Research Department, DCCI

Potential areas of industrial investment

By the end of the 1950s, industry in Dubai started to move slowly from the vocational form to the use of machines; this marked the beginning of the industrial firms in their modern form. Before that era the industry of pearl-fishing boats, fishing as well as craftsmanship in making tools, and equipment used in agriculture, construction and cultivation of lands were almost the only industries in the emirate. In addition there were some other industries, such as manufacturing home appliances, stitching clothes and some other vocational professions, that depended on limited facilities and inherited human expertise rather than on the collective managerial and technical organization that characterize modern industry.

The 1960s saw the beginning of the setting up of modern industrial firms and consequently the emergence of industrial activity as an effective economic sector in society, but the promulgation of Federal Law No. (1) of 1979 concerning the organization of the industrial affairs was the climax of industrial development plans and laid emphasis on the importance and role of the industrial sector. This law defined clearly the nature of an industrial project; it provides that an industrial project is a place equipped with the aim of undertaking one of the following basic operations:

- extraction of raw materials from natural mineral ores and transforming, purifying and preparing them to be marketable products;
- transformation of raw materials according to their substance, components or shape into final products or semi-manufactured products

including mixing, purifying, assembling, forming or packing the products;

- adding a production capacity to an existing industrial project or formation of new production assets to replace old and fully depreciated ones.

The law stipulates that the capital of the project should not be less than AED250,000 and its minimum number of workers should be 10. It should be operated by a power of not less than 5 horsepower. This law and its executive regulations* are considered the most important documents to be studied carefully when embarking upon the study of any industrial project. This is because they determine several aspects that should be taken into consideration, such as procedure for licensing industrial projects, means of their promotion, duties of their owners and penalties that will be inflicted on any person who violates the provisions of the said law and regulations.

The economy of Dubai has witnessed tremendous structural changes in the last two decades. Such transformation has been mostly felt through significant shifts in the pattern of sectoral production. In particular, the fertile environment of a modern infrastructure, efficient financial markets, complete networks of transportation and telecommunication systems, and free-trade-oriented public policy, have been the feeding lines that nourished and nurtured the transformation and increasing depth of Dubai's economy. The most significant change in the emirate's economic base can be clearly visualized by reviewing evidence from the manufacturing sector.

At the country level, the industrial sector in Dubai is considered a driving force of industrial development in the UAE. In 2001, the industrial sector in Dubai produced about 38.8 per cent of the country's manufactured goods. At the emirate level, the industrial sector represents an important element of a diversified economic base, contributing in 2001 about 16 per cent of the emirate's GDP.

* These regulations have been issued by the Ministerial Decision No. (26) of the year 1980 by the Minister of Finance and Industry.

Structural characteristics of Dubai's industrial sector

Scale

At the firm level (the number of firms engaged in that business), the basic metal industry seems to dominate other industries in terms of scale. The scale level of the rest of the industries seems to vary with the adopted scale measure. Using the investment level, the chemicals industry is the highest, as it is when employing the value of production as a scale measure. In terms of the employment scale and that of export value, the ready-made-garment industry leads the others.

Significance

A general feature of structural change within the industrial sector during the last five years is the continual decline in the relative importance of the basic metal industry. Such relative decline is felt with respect to all activities including production, investment, employment and exports. Given the remarkable growth rates achieved by industrial activities during the same period, this indicates greater diversification of the sector's economic base. Development in the sector reveals a rising significance for the basic metal industry in production and employment. Most importantly, using the four measures of significance (production, investment, employment and exports), it is clear that there is a general contraction in the shares of the two leading industries. The basic metal industry signifies industrial diversification.

Export to international markets

In recent years, the superior performance of countries on an export-oriented growth path has been related mainly to a more efficient allocation of resources. This seems to be a strong characteristic of Dubai and, in particular, its industrial sector. Nevertheless, the degree of 'manufacturing for exports' varies among the sector's industries. Industries that produce for the sole purpose of satisfying foreign demand include those focused on textiles and basic metal, while the non-metal products industry produces mainly for the domestic markets.

Production techniques

The intensity of capital use in production can be visualized through the capital:labour ratio. Although the industrial sector's aggregate capital:labour ratio fluctuated significantly over the last five years, great diversity among the industries exists. Capital intensity is highest (and far exceeds that of other industries) in the basic metal industry. Other industries that are relatively capital-intensive include chemicals and non-metal products. Industries that can be characterized as labour-intensive are those dealing with textiles and wood products.

Industrial investment incentives

Dubai enjoys a good geographical location in the middle of two important consumer markets: Asia and Africa. Its modern infrastructure is characterized by well-developed means of transport, a network of roads linking it with all the Gulf Cooperation Council (GCC) countries, an international airport and seaports connecting it with all destinations in the world, in addition to the availability of different means of communications and all types of energy, water, public and sanitary utilities. All these facilities make Dubai an ideal site for industrial investment. Moreover, the government provides the industrial projects with many facilities to strengthen their capability to start practising their production activity. These facilities are:

- *Tax exemption*. National industrial firms are exempted from all taxes and duties levied on profits or production, with the exception of certain administrative fees imposed by the authorities in charge of the licensing and issuing of certificates of origin. There are also no restrictions on profit transfer or capital repatriation.
- *Encouraging incentives*. Imports (machinery, equipment and raw materials) and exports (manufactured or semi-manufactured products) for industrial projects are exempted from customs duties. Industrial projects are exempted from customs duties on the basis of a letter signed by the Ministry of Finance and Industry, in accordance with the Ministerial Resolution No. (25) of the year 1985 (issued by the Minister of Finance and Industry and the Cabinet's Resolution No. (538/28) for the year 1980), provided that the exempted machines and materials shall be used for production purposes and that the firm is inscribed in the Industrial Register of the Industrial Department.

The government, through its competent agencies, provides the necessary promotion and encouragement by holding trade fairs and issuing commercial and industrial directories and other introductory booklets and brochures aimed at acquainting the consumers or the marketing firms inside and outside the country with industrial firms and their products.

In a step intended to support business sectors and boost industrial activities in Dubai, the Crown Prince of Dubai and UAE Minister of Defence, General HH Sheikh Mohammed bin Rashid Al Maktoum, issued a decree in August 1999 exempting manufacturing firms from fees paid to the Dubai Chamber of Commerce and Industry as well as other local departments. The decree does not include firms operating in the free zones.

Price preference

As per the rules and conditions issued by Ministerial Decree No. 13 of 1986 (concerning the rules of granting price preference in the government purchases) and Ministerial Decree No. 51 of 1986 (concerning the exclusive procedure for granting price preference), national industrial products are given a 10 per cent price advantage in government purchases over imported goods. These rules and conditions are as follows:

- *Conditions for giving price preference.* The industrial firm must be inscribed in the Industrial Register at the Industrial Department. The firm must have a valid industrial licence issued by the Economic Development Department. The contribution of the UAE nationals to the paid-up capital should not be less than 51 per cent. The added value resulting from the manufacture of the product should not be less than 40 per cent of its final value. The paid-up capital should not be less than AED250,000.
- *Regulations for granting price preference.* Quality and promptness of delivery are to be considered. For the purpose of price preference, prices are calculated on the basis of the lower price. In case the quality of the foreign and the local products is technically equal, the criterion of preference is applied in favour of the local product, even if its price is higher by 10 per cent than the price of the foreign product. In cases where the local commodities are competitive with the foreign ones in quality and price, the tender should be awarded to the local commodities without price preference. If the local commodities are competitive in quality with the foreign commodities but their prices are higher by more than 10 per cent, the tender is awarded to the foreign commodities supplier.

Industrial areas planning

The government has also allocated a number of places as industrial areas and provided them with all the necessary services, such as internal roads, power and water supplies, communications, telecommunications and other services. The most important industrial areas in Dubai that can accommodate new industrial projects are:

- *Ras Al Khor Industrial Area*. The Ras Al Khor Industrial Area is the newest among the industrial areas. Its area is 661 hectares, which has been allocated to accommodate small and medium-sized industrial activities. In this area it is allowed to set up warehouses besides small or medium-sized workshops, carpentry workshops, furniture factories and other industrial projects that have no contamination effects on the environment.
- *Al-Qouz Industrial Area*. This area is considered an ideal place for setting up all kinds of industrial activities. Its total area is 1,838 hectares and factories operating in this area vary from light to heavy industries. There are also warehouse and labour quarters to accommodate those who work in these factories. This area is still capable of accommodating any new industrial projects whether they are medium-sized or heavy industries.
- *Al Safa Area*. This area is allocated to accommodate industries related to the production of consumer foodstuffs. There is a possibility that it will be expanded to accommodate new industries. Its total area is about 20 hectares.
- *Al Khubaisi Area*. This area is planned to be up to 102 hectares. It is allocated to contain warehouses, workshops, light industry projects and some trading activities. Al Khubaisi area has a special economic importance particularly to trading firms located in the centre of the town, because it is nearby and has many facilities for storing goods. There is no possibility to shift this area to another location in the near future. New industrial projects can be set up in this area, especially those projects that do not have negative effects on the public health and the environment.
- *Um-Ramool Industrial Area*. This area is planned to cover 391 hectares. It accommodates warehouses, workshops and different industries. Some of its main roads have been converted to trading roads near which showrooms can be established. It is permitted to establish different industrial projects except heavy industrial projects.

- *Al-Qusais Industrial Area.* Its total area is 545 hectares. It is set to accommodate medium- and small-sized industrial projects that have no negative effects on the environment. Industrial activities practised in this total area of 545 hectares are divided into block factories, contracting companies and gas storage. An area of 65 hectares each is allocated for activities related to construction contracting and metal scrap collection. The rest of the area is allocated to set up small and medium-sized industrial projects that have no negative effects on the environment.
- *Jebel Ali Industrial Area.* Setting up industries in Jebel Ali started even before establishment of the Jebel Ali Free Zone in 1985. All companies in Jebel Ali, whether within or outside of the free zone, enjoy the advantage of being adjacent to the Jebel Ali sea port. Within the free zone there are over 300 industrial units, which represent about 20 per cent of the total forms operating in Jebel Ali. These factories enjoy plenty of benefits and advantages including spacious and cheap warehousing facilities.

Industrial services

The Dubai government has endeavoured to extend the services required for practising industrial activities in those industrial areas. The rates of some of these services are very competitive compared with the rates of similar services in the industrialized countries. Table 3.1.1. shows the prevailing charges of the important industrial services, which are necessary for operation and production.

Table 3.1.1. Prices of industrial services in Dubai

Item	Unit	Current cost	
		AED	US$
Stores and warehouses (rental)	Sq. metre	146	40
Stores and warehouses (constructed)	Sq. metre	450	123
Pre-built factory units (rental)	Sq. metre	183	50
Pre-built factory units (constructed)	Sq. metre	500	136
Rent of offices	Sq. metre	550	150
Construction of office buildings	Sq. metre	1,350	368
Rent of service areas (car parking)	Sq. metre	55	15
Rent of industrial plots	Sq. metre	5.38	1.45

Item	Unit	Current cost	
		AED	US$
Utility cost			
Electricity	Kw/h	0.200	0.054
Water for industrial operations	Cubic metre	6.600	1.798
Gasoline			
High octane	Litre	0.870	0.319
Low octane	Litre	0.803	0.295
Natural gas	1,000 Cubic Ft	7.500	2.000

Exchange rate: US$1=AED 3.67

Possible investment opportunities in industrial projects

Activity of the industrial sector

In 2002 the number of the existing industrial firms in Dubai stood at about 1,000. They were producing several kinds of commodities, consumer goods, building materials metal products and some industrial equipment. Table 3.1.2 shows the number of factories in Dubai according to their industrial sector between 1998 and 2002, while Table 3.1.3 shows the volume of industrial production during 1998–2002.

Table 3.1.2. Development of factories in Dubai 1998–2002

Classification No.	Division name	No. of factories				
		1998	1999	2000	2001	2002
15	Manufacture of food products and beverages	89	91	98	102	106
16	Manufacture of tobacco products	1	2	2	3	4
17	Manufacture of textiles	19	19	21	21	22
18	Manufacture of wearing apparel	27	30	30	32	32

Classification No.	Division name	No. of factories				
		1998	**1999**	**2000**	**2001**	**2002**
19	Manufacture of leather products	5	5	5	5	5
20	Manufacture of wood and products of wood	14	15	16	17	21
21	Manufacture of paper and paper products	37	37	37	40	40
22	Publishing and printing	39	40	40	40	43
23	Manufacture of refined petroleum products	5	5	7	8	10
24	Manufacture of chemicals and chemical products	62	68	76	85	93
25	Manufacture of rubber and plastic products	49	53	58	64	66
26	Manufacture of non-metallic mineral products	93	96	99	106	107
27	Manufacture of basic metals	15	17	19	20	23
28	Manufacture of fabricated metal products	165	170	182	191	207
29	Manufacture of machinery and equipment	20	24	27	28	34
30	Manufacture of office, accounting and computing machinery	1	3	4	4	4
31	Manufacture of electrical machinery apparatus	30	31	36	37	41
32	Manufacture of radio, TV, communication equipment and apparatus	1	1	1	2	2
33	Manufacture of scientific and professional instruments	2	2	2	2	2
34	Manufacture of motor vehicles, trailers and semi-trailers	10	11	12	12	12
35	Manufacture of other transport equipment	28	31	32	32	36
36	Manufacture of furniture and manufacturing NEC	58	61	70	80	84

Classification No.	Division name	No. of factories				
		1998	1999	2000	2001	2002
37	Recycling	6	6	6	6	6
	Total	**776**	**818**	**880**	**937**	**1,000**

*covers only factories registered with DCCI

Source: Membership Department, DCCI

Table 3.1.3. Development of industrial production value 1998–2002

Classification No.	Division name	No. of factories				
		1998	1999	2000	2001	2002
15	Manufacture of food products and beverages	2,249	2,917	2,919	3,084	3,455
16	Manufacture of tobacco products	6	17	50	45	44
17	Manufacture of textiles	460	537	584	576	518
18	Manufacture of wearing apparel	525	699	659	745	793
19	Manufacture of leather products	70	80	83	155	155
20	Manufacture of wood and products of wood	19	137	117	194	249
21	Manufacture of paper and paper products	450	638	637	695	765
22	Publishing and printing	176	678	676	704	707
23	Manufacture of refined petroleum products	2,197	2,201	2,201	2,262	1,479
24	Manufacture of chemicals and chemicals products	952	1,303	1,427	1,490	1,639
25	Manufacture of rubber and plastic products	568	833	1,046	1,094	1,144

Classification No.	Division name	No. of factories				
		1998	1999	2000	2001	2002
26	Manufacture of non-metallic mineral Products	182	2,182	2,011	1,856	1,831
27	Manufacture of basic metals	3,083	4,011	3,211	3,965	4,037
28	Manufacture of fabricated metal products	2,999	3,985	2,963	2,957	5,118
29	Manufacture of machinery and equipment	173	211	308	284	409
30	Manufacture of office, accounting and computing machinery	52	46	58	68	70
31	Manufacture of electrical machinery apparatus	268	630	863	1,046	970
32	Manufacture of radio, TV, communication equipment and apparatus	4	3	3	11	11
33	Manufacture of scientific and professional instruments	9	9	10	7	13
34	Manufacture of motor vehicles, trailers and semi-trailers	56	80	120	107	109
35	Manufacture of other transport equipment	1,861	1,716	1,686	1,665	1,714
36	Manufacture of furniture and manufacturing NEC	161	447	484	583	640
37	Recycling	86	100	100	86	78
	Total	**16,606**	**23,460**	**22,216**	**23,679**	**25,948**

*covers industries operating in the Jebel Ali Free Zone

Source: Membership Department, DCCI

Feasible industrial investment areas

Despite the varied production areas of the existing industrial firms, opportunities still exist for more investments in the industrial sector, to produce many commodities that can meet the market needs and the various tastes of the consumers, as well as find a good market whether that be in the UAE, GCC countries or even internationally. No doubt, choosing a suitable industrial area depends, above all, on the selection of a new production activity that would satisfy the consumer's need for either new commodities that are not produced locally by the existing industrial firms, or on the selection of a production activity that can meet the volume of consumption of a local product, which existing industrial firms cannot cover. In both cases, the products should be of high quality according to international standard specifications, so that they can compete in the market with similar imported products. These matters should be taken into consideration while preparing the technical and economic feasibility study of any project.

It is worth mentioning that the area of production of any project to be set up should conform with UAE industrial development policies and plans, taking into consideration the following:

- economic and social demands as well as industrial development programmes of the UAE;
- consumers' demands and the need to replace locally manufactured products with imported items at cheaper cost;
- emphasis on industries that depend on local raw materials for the manufacture of final products or intermediate products that are marketed locally or can also be marketed abroad;
- capital-intensive projects, introducing modern technology;
- projects that can be set up in the industrial areas as decided by the government, that comply with technical and health requirements and that are environmentally friendly.

As yet there are no feasibility studies available at the competent government departments of the best investment areas in the industrial sector. However, due to the free investment policy pursued by the government to give the investor the freedom of choosing the appropriate area, it should be mentioned that possible investment opportunities that have good chances of success crop up in the following areas:

- garment and textile, processing and dyeing and yarn industry;
- drugs, medical bandages, cosmetics and pharmaceutical industry;
- spare parts for cars and electronic devices especially starters, cooling regulators, ignition plugs and oil filters;
- canning of foodstuffs and beverages, especially fish and other sea-foods, industries related to date processing and palm-tree products, bee honey production and other products related to food security policies;
- polyvinyl acetate products used as a basic substance for manufacturing paints; acrylic resins used for coating and insulating buildings and metals; steel, magnesium and aluminium solvents used for water desalination, paper production, textiles, fertilizers and industrial chemicals;
- paper production by pneumatic methods and polystyrene substances for packaging;
- production of different sizes of batteries with their accessories;
- gas cookers, washing machines, refrigerators, other household appliances and dehumidifiers;
- office equipment and furniture, especially personal computers;
- sports equipment and apparatus;
- production of building materials such as gates, fences, barriers and aluminium and copper manufactured by casting methods such as locks, handles, brass panels for doors, locks with handles, copper and aluminium joints, bathroom sets made of artificial marble and light concrete roofing bricks.

Procedure for licensing industrial projects

Only firms owned wholly by UAE or GCC nationals can obtain a licence for setting up an industrial project, with the exception of companies in which the contribution of the national capital is not less than 51 per cent. In this case, the managing director of the company should be a national as should the majority of the members of the board of directors. When these conditions are fulfilled the procedure for licensing industrial projects takes the following steps:

1. obtaining the initial approval from the Ministry of Finance and Industry;
2. obtaining the industrial licence from the Economic Development Department;
3. registration with the Dubai Chamber of Commerce and Industry;
4. inscription of the project in the Industrial Register at the Industrial Department and obtaining an Industrial Production Licence.

3.2

Dubai Agricultural Sector

Data Management and Business Research Department, DCCI

Possibilities and areas of investment in the agricultural sector

The emirate of Dubai is not considered as agricultural because the cultivated area is less than 19 per cent of the total area of the emirate and most of it is located in the middle of the country. There are also additional reasons why it is difficult to increase agricultural production:

- The agricultural production constitutes only 1.6 per cent of the GDP.
- The share of agricultural activities in Dubai has amounted to 0.5 per cent of the total number of people working in different business sectors. This figure is low as many individuals shifted to modern activities after the discovery of oil and the development of commercial activities and social services such as education, medical services and housing among others.
- There are some difficulties that hinder the development of agricultural activity in Dubai, such as insufficient water for irrigation which prevents the use of around 21,506 donums of land that could be cultivated.
- The sand soil of plains whose area constitutes 93 per cent of the total area of the emirate is one of the obstacles to the development efforts made by the government and individuals. This matter necessitates a precise study of the areas of investment in this sector.

Agricultural areas in Dubai

Some simple types of agriculture – that, essentially, depend on planting palm trees, some types of citrus trees, vegetables and animal fodder – are concentrated in the areas listed below.

Al Awir

This area is 25 kilometres from Dubai city and contains 68 per cent of the total number of the farms and 77 per cent of the total cultivated area. This area measures 47,373 donums and includes the areas of Mushref, Al Khawanij and Hibab.

Hatta

This area is 100 kilometres from the city of Dubai, near the borders of Oman. It comes after Al Awir in terms of importance. It contains 426 farms or 33 per cent of the number of farms in the emirate and, measuring 6,591 donums, constitutes 11 per cent of the total area of the emirate.

Area of Dubai: Al Ain Road

This area is 40 kilometres from the city of Dubai. It is located along Al Ain Road. It contains some vegetable farms and palm and fruit trees, in addition to some livestock and dairy projects. The areas of Al Rawieh, Al Liseeli, Maraqab and Kretisseh are included in this area.

Food security projects

Although the share of the agricultural sector in the GDP of Dubai is small, the concerned authorities are endeavouring to boost agricultural production as much as possible through increasing the green area by cultivating new lands or using modern technology to improve production. The aim is to meet the population needs for agricultural, animal and fish products in order to reduce the pressures of a food security problem, which is an aggravating concern in times of political crises. The emirate of Dubai does not differ from the other emirates of the state in its large dependence on imports for meeting its food needs. The average rate of self-sufficiency of the UAE regarding white meat is 24 per cent, 26 per cent regarding red meat and 36 per cent regarding eggs. This rate has, however, reached 100 per cent for fish and dates.

Agricultural production

The government plans for increasing the agricultural area have met with success through encouraging the possession of agricultural lands. The local agricultural production was almost zero; the area of cultivated land has increased noticeably since that time. Table 3.2.1 shows the development of the number of farms and cultivated areas in the emirate during 1999–2003.

Table 3.2.1. The number of farms and cultivated areas in Dubai 1999–2003

Year	No. of farms	Total area (donums)	Cultivated area (donums)	Uncultivated area (donums)
1999	1,240	53,805	51,139	2,666
2000	1,268	57,181	54,577	2,604
2001	1,277	61,689	59,087	2,602
2002	1,300	61,775	59,193	2,582
2003	1,326	61,757	59,171	2,586

Source: Ministry of Agriculture and Fisheries

Table 3.2.2 shows the quantity of the agricultural production in 2003 of vegetables, fruits and other farm products.

Table 3.2.2. Quantity of the agricultural production in Dubai for 2003

Crop	Cultivated area (donums)	Production quantity (tonnes)	Production value (AED'000)
Vegetables	1,159	2,137	3,546
Fruit trees	17,040	16,519	55,938
Field crop	6,912	46,418	62,144
Total	**25,111**	**65,074**	**121,628**

Source: Ministry of Agriculture and Fisheries

Animal wealth

There are seven poultry farms in Dubai; their annual production amounts to 6,479 tonnes of chicken meat. There are also five farms for breeding cows and dairy production where the number of cows exceeds 3,718 used in producing fresh milk, a part of which is used in dairy products. Table 3.2.3 shows the number of livestock farms and the volume of their production from 1999 to 2003.

Table 3.2.3. Number of poultry and dairy farms and production 1999–2003

Particulars	1999	2000	2001	2002	2003
Farms	6	7	7	7	7
Chicks production ('000)	9,993	6,340	6,479	6,238	10,366
Cow farms	5	5	5	5	5
Cows	3,945	5,123	5,957	5,957	5,957
Milk production (tonnes)	18,514	31,928	34,514	41,340	39,108

Source: Ministry of Agriculture and Fisheries

Fishing

Eight ports have been allocated for fishing in Dubai. They are Jumeirah Port 1, Jumeirah 3, Jumeirah 6, Khor Dubai, Ras Al Khor, Al Hamriyah, Al Jaddaf and Ghantout. Fishing is practised in the Arabian Gulf, which is calm almost all year round. The quantity of fish sold in both Deira and Bur Dubai markets is about 21,000 tonnes per annum. Furthermore, the number of fishermen in the emirate is 2,379, representing 18.5 per cent of the total number of fishermen in the UAE. The number of fishing boats is 692, which represents 15 per cent of the fishing boats in the country.

Agricultural services and facilities

The Ministry of Agriculture and Fisheries provides the agricultural sector with a series of services and facilities. These are outlined in brief below:

- agricultural sector:
  - levelling and ploughing services;
  - facilities granted in the form of production requirements;
  - establishing model farms to train the farmers and the workers in the agricultural sector;
  - providing agricultural extension services to farmers.
- animal sector:
  - modern services to immunize animals against diseases and epidemics and undertaking surgical operations for animals;
  - establishing artificial insemination centres.
- fisheries sector:
  - providing loans in kind related to production needs;
  - services of repairing the machinery and fishing boats;
  - training and guiding the fishermen to practise the fishing career;
  - establishing Mari-culture research centres and production of fish larve to enrich fish stock.
- water and soil:
  - services of teaching the farmers ways of better use of irrigation water and avoiding water wastage;
  - guiding the farmers to the modern methods of irrigation;
  - designing and preparing technical specifications to construct a number of dams for increasing the quantity of irrigation water.
- health and veterinary quarantine:
  - establishing agricultural and veterinary quarantine centres at the ports of the country, in order to protect local products against overseas diseases;

- undertaking health inspection on agricultural and animal exports in order to maintain the good reputation of the UAE exports;
- examining agricultural production requirements when they enter the country and their impact on the agricultural structure.

- laboratories and scientific analysis:
  - The Ministry of Agriculture and Fisheries has set up the central laboratory for undertaking scientific research and analysis of water and soil samples and medical analysis on animals.
  - many tests were made on water and soil to ensure their suitability for drinking and irrigation.
  - the Ministry has contributed to applying scientific methods in agriculture and animal breeding.
  - the Ministry has contributed to the protection of the environment, animals and human beings against common diseases.

Possible investment opportunities in agricultural projects

The investment projects in the agricultural sector arise from the actual needs of the UAE. These needs are normally mentioned in the economic plans set by the UAE planning authorities. Thus, it is appropriate to mention here the areas relating to land cultivation and increasing the area of land used for agriculture; drilling wells for extracting water; providing machinery and agricultural equipment; developing the fishing fleet; undertaking research, studies and agricultural consultancies; and establishing joint ventures that undertake different agricultural services in order to increase the productivity of the agricultural sector. Whereas there are no ready economic studies on possible investment projects in the emirate, general indicators can be given to such projects on which feasibility studies may be conducted such as:

- Establishment of new agricultural projects to produce field crops and fruits and vegetables of economic quality, which are suitable to the prevailing climatic conditions and the possibility of marketing them locally or exporting them abroad, including the protected agriculture.

- Enlarging the existing agricultural activities in the field of animal and chicken breeding, producing animal fodder, fish breeding, expanding fishing and developing fisheries outside the Gulf zone.
- Establishment of agricultural projects that depend on exporting agricultural products to European countries in seasons when the European production of such products is reduced, taking into consideration the quality of packing, quick delivery and other important marketing factors to raise the investment revenue of the projects. Some of those projects are growing vegetables and some types of fruits.

Procedure for licensing agricultural projects

The establishment of agricultural projects in Dubai is licensed to firms owned wholly by UAE nationals, the nationals of GCC countries or to companies in which the contribution of the national capital is not less than 51 per cent. When these conditions are fulfilled the procedure for licensing agricultural projects takes the following steps:

1. obtaining an agricultural licence from the Department of Economic Development;
2. registering with the Dubai Chamber of Commerce and Industry.

3.3

Infrastructure and Commerce

Data Management and Business Research Department, DCCI

Investment incentives

Appropriate infrastructure is considered one of the most important investment incentives in any commercial sector. This means integrating the different elements of infrastructure in such an efficient manner that the needs of commercial activity regarding swift effectiveness and accuracy are met. These elements should be well equipped and to the latest international standards, in addition to keeping pace with the developments and changes witnessed by the modern world in that field. Moreover, the infrastructural elements are distinguished by their capacity to accommodate high levels of activity that leave no chance for jamming, delay or substandard performance.

The custom duties levied on goods and commodities passing through sea and air ports of Dubai are considered the lowest in the world; furthermore, some goods, such as foodstuffs, raw material used in industry, gold, building material and others, are even exempted from these duties. This helps in keeping the rates of such goods and commodities fixed, to a great extent, when they are re-exported. Also, the goods in transit or that are imported for the purpose of re-export can be landed and stored for certain periods before re-export without any customs duty needing to be paid.

The several seaports, in addition to the international airport, which are designed according to high international standards, have made Dubai the landing point for tens of international airlines and shipping lines to the extent that, through a network of air and maritime lines, it is easily connected, almost at any time, to hundreds of cities and ports all around the world. This feature is reflected positively and distinctively on the efficiency of the commercial activities.

The above mentioned elements have a positive effect on the cost of transportation and shipment of goods and commodities, for such cost in Dubai is considered one of the lowest known worldwide. Such incentives are favourable to the mixed shipments to Europe and the USA and vice versa, which, no doubt, help to stabilize prices of goods in the market and consequently make them more competitive.

Dubai markets enjoy a historical reputation due to its geographical location, which enabled it to be the pioneer of commercial activity in the Gulf region. This reputation is such that it is possible to say that Dubai markets represent international exhibitions that run throughout the year and are successful for many reasons, such as:

- Dubai is characterized by its specialized markets, which are gathered almost in one spot, so that we find garment and textile markets, electronic and electric appliance markets, furniture markets, home appliances markets and others in the same place.
- These markets exhibit vast collections of goods and commodities imported from almost all parts of the world, which makes the purchaser's choice large and suitable to his/her purchasing power.
- The visitors to these markets come from all countries of the region, where they meet and complete their deals. Some of them simply purchase what is readily available and some place orders for a future supply of the goods they require.

The commercial activities react in such a manner that they often feed from each other: the rise of the retail and wholesale trade affects the real-estate sector, which consequently affects the construction and building sector, while all of these activities affect the banking activity, insurance and other related services. So, it moves in a complete and balanced circle that results in opening and developing new areas of opportunities and possibilities for those interested in being a part of this non-stop activity.

Commercial sectors liable for investment

Construction and building sector

The construction and building sector is considered to be one of the commercial sectors that developed along with the discovery of oil and utilization of oil revenues in setting up the infrastructure and the social and economic utilities. This occurred along with the changes that took place due to the inflow of foreign manpower and exposure to the outside world, which resulted in essential changes in the social and economic fields. Such influence was noticeable and tangible in the construction and building sector, this being the physical aspect of the development achieved in the other fields.

Possible investment opportunities
There are still many investment opportunities in the construction and building sector, and among those which have a good chance of success are:

- joint ventures between national contracting companies and international firms that enjoy a good reputation for executing specialized construction projects and entering the field of regional and international competition;
- contracting companies specialized in executing residential premises provided they have high technical capabilities to execute such projects at excellent levels of performance;
- companies that undertake partially specialized contracting provided that they acquire high technical capabilities to execute different works such as laying foundations, carrying out cement works, paint works, carpentry works, laying of tiles and marble, fixtures, air-conditioning works, mechanical equipment and others;
- establishments specialized in interior design works, decoration and ornamentation, wallpaper works, landscaping and improving interior and exterior yards with natural and artificial views, construction of swimming pools and others.

Retail and wholesale trade

Dubai's domestic trade was prosperous even before the discovery and exploitation of oil resources due to its strategic and distinctive geographical location. However, the abundance and increase of capital after the discovery of oil largely helped to pave the way for market expansion. This also made available investment opportunities in the trade exchange in all aspects under the prevailing free trade policy and special characteristics. This occurred, primarily, because the quantities of goods and commodities imported by Dubai are not due to its need for such imports, but to meet the needs of the its neighbouring markets. Such volume of imports is considered to be somewhat self-financing for it leads to the reduction of the unit price so that it is possible to re-export the goods without an essential increase in actual price. Moreover, many merchants in Dubai still follow the barter method and collect the value of their goods in the form of other goods.

The traditional style of trade, such as trading in dates, dried fish, spices, agricultural crops, gold, pearls, perfumes and similar items, dominated most of the commodities dealt with in the wholesale and retail markets. However, with the era of oil and economic and social development, the merchants shifted their operations to modern consumer goods and commodities whether imported from abroad or produced locally. Also, due to modern communication capabilities and easy trade dealings, the scope of the trade exchange exceeded the Gulf countries, India and the East African coast and spread to the whole world.

Western European countries, Japan, the USA and GCC states are considered to be the major countries with which foreign trade has been enhanced. Also these countries have been keen to establish trade representative centres and offices in Dubai to the extent that their number reached 54 government trade centres (liaison offices), 247 trade representative offices for international trading firms, 20 business councils for promoting business relations and eight regional liaison offices.

Trade-related services

There are many establishments of major importance to commercial activities, namely those that conduct different types of trade-related services and activities. These include agents of purchasing goods who sell them on commission; trade brokers; auction sale halls; advertising agencies; weighing and measuring services; those who issue, sell and replace trade cards and provide other commercial services.

Repair services

Repair services include firms that provide repair and maintenance services for heavy equipment, household items, electrical appliances, refrigerators, washing machines, irons and vacuum cleaners. They also include workshops for maintenance of all kinds of vehicles, light and heavy, as well as other consumer products.

Hotels and restaurants

The first hotel in Dubai was built in 1961. Now the number of hotels in Dubai and the standard and quality of services provided by them have qualified the emirate to be a centre for business and tourism. The various standard hotel indicators show the rise in tourist activity in the emirate of Dubai during the period between 1999 and 2003 (Table 3.3.1).

Table 3.3.1. Development of tourism activity in Dubai 1999–2003

Details	Year				
	1999	2000	2001	2002	2003
Number of hotels	254	265	264	272	271
Number of rooms	18,638	20,315	21,248	23,170	25,571
Number of beds	31,267	33,364	35,483	38,386	41,226
Room occupancy (%)	59	61.2	60.9	70.2	72.4
Bed occupancy (%)	53.8	57.9	57.2	64.3	67.6
Number of guests	2,480,821	2,835,638	3,064,701	4,107,236	4,342,341
Nights stayed	5,854,375	7,117,451	7,185,837	8,937,758	10,290,710
Hotels revenues (AED'000)	2,228,074	2,662,233	2,792,096	3,409,726	4,016,075

Source: Ministry of Planning, Department of Economic Development, Department of Tourism and Commerce Marketing

During 2003 Dubai's hotels hosted the majority of guests in the UAE. Guests from Europe constituted 17.5 per cent of the total guests in Dubai's hotels; Asian and African visitors formed 23.7 per cent. However, the largest number of guests was from GCC countries, accounting for almost 29.5 per cent of the total guests in Dubai's hotels. American tourists formed only 3.1 per cent of the total.

There are lot of restaurants, cafeterias and outlets offering various kinds of food and beverages. The advancement in the tourist sector was instrumental in raising the number and type of such restaurants and coffee shops, particularly in five-star and first-class hotels. Yet, opportunities are still there for investment in the restaurant and fast-food outlet business. Old restaurants and cafeterias observe strict hygiene rules laid down by the Dubai Municipality. The Municipality inspectors regularly launch field campaigns to ensure that health regulations are complied with by the food- and beverage-selling outlets.

Transportation and storage

The transport means are considered one of the major important trade elements that enhanced the prosperity of commercial activity in Dubai, because the construction of the internal and external highways that connect Dubai with the other emirates, together with the construction of modern seaports such as Port Rashid and Jebel Ali Port in addition to Dubai International Airport, have doubled the possibilities of commercial activity and made Dubai one of the important transportation and shipping centres in the region. This was particularly so after the large expansion of Dubai International Airport, which expects to receive 30 million passengers by 2010. In addition, adding the cargo village to the airport made Dubai an international centre for both sea and air cargo.

Land transportation

The history of modern land transport in Dubai started in 1932 when the first company was established with a modest fleet consisting of five vehicles. The growth of the transport sector was slow until the middle of the 1950s when the establishment of public transport companies started to increase. Until the beginning of the 1960s the scope of land transport was very limited due to the tough nature of the roads and the confinement of land transport services to inside the cities for the most part. Along with the increase of commercial and industrial development and the expansion of services firms during the 1970s, this sector started to develop rapidly to keep pace with these changes in order to set up and develop the infrastructure in Dubai and the other emirates.

The transport sector, gradually but within a relatively short period of time, shifted from contributing to the transportation of raw materials required to construct the infrastructure to the ideal use of such infrastructure. Consequently it played an active role in transporting goods to local markets and then to the regional markets in the GCC countries – hence the rate of trade dealings increased between Dubai, the other emirates and the GCC countries.

GCC countries are considered a natural extension of the UAE markets, particularly after the implementation of the Unified Economic Agreement of the GCC States. The formation of the GCC resulted in the number of the establishments operating in the public transportation sector increasing to 886 firms with a fleet consisting of thousands of trucks. These firms handle the operations of internal and regional transport and cargo and, hence, ascertained their increasing importance in facilitating and activating the commercial activities between Dubai and the other emirates as well as the neighbouring Gulf countries, which are connected through a modern comprehensive network of roads.

Sea transport

Dubai ports are considered the leading ports in the region, which keep pace with the rapid development in the sea transportation industry in view of the modern methods adopted for loading and unloading activities. In view of the strategic location of the emirate, Dubai facilitates cargo handling at its various ports allowing both the ship-owners and the shippers constantly to enjoy the stability of ports' charges.

Another fact that contributed to the efficiency of port services is the recent introduction of computer systems to organize the containers and unload berths with as few procedural formalities and delays as possible. This has been achieved due to streamlining the operations and increasing their efficiency to maintain competitiveness among shipping companies. Perhaps this is the main reason why many of shipping companies, sea transport agents and clearing agents make Dubai the centre of sea-transport operations. There are many maritime lines conducting all kinds of shipping operations and thousands of shippers use Dubai ports because of the appropriate facilities provided, such as bridge cranes, towing of vessels, tug boats, low-load trailers and forklifts, in addition to the possibility of re-exporting the imported goods without the need for getting the goods out of the ports into Dubai city before reloading.

Air transport

Investors are encouraged to establish regional branches and travel agencies in the UAE to meet the requirements of the increasing number of passengers and volume of air cargo. The current agencies represent a large number of international airlines that find good business in Dubai's markets; this business occurs as a result of the facilities and advantages available for conducting all regular air-transport operations and internal and external commercial air services under the 'open space' policy, which was adopted by the Dubai government.

Storage

Dubai has paid great attention to storage facilities by building 22 sheds for covered storage in Port Rashid, and by also providing open storage places and sails at the Jebel Ali Port.

- *Jebel Ali Port.* Covered warehouses: 90,080 square metres; open storage area: 377,480 square metres;
- *Rashid Ports.* Covered warehouses: 58,480 square metres; open storage area: 307,810 square metres.

Real-estate and renting sector

During the last 10 years, the real-estate market witnessed a great demand in buying and selling all kinds of land and properties as a result of the rise in their prices, which were affected by positive economic factors. Land in residential areas increased in value to varying degrees based on location and the possibility of benefiting from the construction of multistorey buildings. The price of land is not only determined by its location, but also by the conditions of building thereon; for example, land upon which multistorey buildings are permitted should have a higher market value than land that doesn't allow for such construction.

The rise of investments in the real-estate sector has led to establishing many companies that render various services that were previously unfamiliar; such services include buying and selling land, residential units and commercial shops, or renting them. These companies manage residential and real-estate projects in accordance with the conditions agreed upon between themselves and the landlords, or by playing the role of agent with regard to renting, buying, evaluating, selling or managing properties or simply extending consultancy services related to the real-estate industry.

It is worth mentioning that investing in this sector by buying commercial, residential or agricultural property is confined to UAE and GCC citizens only. Management and consultancy services of these properties are, however, available to any investor.

Trends in real-estate investment

Real-estate expansion in Dubai is subject in all cases to commercial and industrial development. This means that the establishment of a new commercial or industrial firm consequently leads to the demand for a showroom or a building with certain specifications as well as several houses for the staff of that firm. Therefore, the increased demand for houses presently witnessed in Dubai comes as a result of many reasons, such as:

- the rise in commercial activity, particularly in import and re-export operations, and the engagement of new investors in the trading sector due to the favourable investment climate;
- the increase in the number of establishments and companies that started to operate in Jebel Ali Free Zone – these now number more than 2,300;
- the new residential and commercial buildings can offer attractive services, such as recreational facilities, security (watchman

and camera system), electronic car park system, laundry service, in-house supermarkets etc).

The trends of house rents depend, in all cases, on supply and demand law. It is expected that the demand on commercial and residential buildings will increase within the next two years, in line with the currently expanding commercial and industrial activities in Dubai.

3.4

Consulting and Business Services

Data Management and Business Research Department, DCCI

Legal and accounting consultancy services

With the development of the commercial and civil relationships that are dominating the social life, and with the introduction of issues that have started to become complicated from time to time – especially when the government has issued laws and rules regulating commercial, economic and social affairs – the need for new services on legal issues became an urgent requirement to meet the increased demand for such services. For this purpose, specialized offices and firms have started to act on behalf of clients in commercial and civil cases presented before the courts, as well as offices and establishments operating in the field of consultancy and legal studies for legal problems in which they are not allowed to plead before the courts.

Firms that render accounting services related to book-keeping, auditing and submission of accounting consultancy have also appeared. The presence of such firms has become necessary after the recent developments in the commercial and financial sector and the emergence of accountancy awareness. These firms will provide services such as the preparation of statements that show the establishments' financial position, profit and loss accounts to be presented to the shareholders or to the authorities, or help in obtaining credit and banking facilities.

Engineering and architectural consultancy services

The boost in construction and building activities was the real starting point of specialized engineering and architectural services. Furthermore, some of the small firms that prepare engineering drawings have been converted into important companies to design constructional projects and prepare engineering plans. There was also a new stage of preparing engineering and architectural studies and of engineering specialization in constructional and architectural consultancy. Such activity was crowned by the issue of the legislation organizing the aspects of practising the profession of engineering consultancy in the emirate. Thus there are many firms operating in the field of, among others:

- studies and designs preparation;
- drawings;
- engineering consultancy and specifications related to roads, bridges, tunnels, water drainage, landscaping, power stations, housing, commercial and industrial buildings, and public buildings such as hospitals, schools;
- electrical and mechanical consulting engineering;
- mining;
- industrial engineering.

The existence of these services has led to the creation of other subsidiary firms that prepare drawings and aerial photographs related to town planning and studying the adequate systems in terms of traffic, water drainage and management of constructional projects.

Technical services and consultancy

The impact of the new lifestyle has extended to include all aspects of economic activity. Therefore, the market has witnessed the emergence of some specialized firms rendering different technical consultancy services such as specialized agricultural studies on land reclamation, pest control, fertilization, livestock and poultry breeding. Firms have been established that provide geological services, geotechnical studies and related data analysis, together with those specialized in submitting industrial studies and advice on the various technical and technological aspects related to machinery and equipment use and maintenance, factory planning, commodity design, factory operation and production design. This is in addition to firms specialized in oil and natural gas, metals, natural resources and underground water exploration, who prepare studies, reports and related technical studies without extending their activities to exploit these resources. Also included are firms specialized in the design of applied systems for the use of computers, programming, installing computer software as well as testing, operating, maintaining and training thereon.

Administrative and economic services and consultancy

The business sector has always made great impact on all economic sectors and provided an incentive to upgrade the efficiency of economic activity. It is also considered the indicator of prosperity and a measure of economic trends. Therefore, it is natural to find firms specialized in managerial and economic services such as those that offer feasibility studies and prepare technical and economic studies for new projects.

There are also firms that offer managerial training services and operate in the field of staff training to upgrade the efficiency and performance in certain management areas such as accountancy, sales, marketing and advertising skills. These firms work together with those specializing in financial investments, insurance, real estate, insurance claims settlements, loss adjustment, and damage and compensation estimating. There are also firms working in advertising and production, design broadcast, television, movie cassettes or producing the same in the form of signs and posters for newspapers and magazines. This is in addition to those firms specialized in offering other works that include photocopying; management of companies/establishments; documents clearing; business administration; secretarial, employment and recruitment services; exhibition organization; book publishing; advertising; gifts supply and other administrative and economic services related to the business sector.

Planning and statistical database

The municipality prepares the planning and statistical database by gathering information from the investors, the local and federal departments, and from related studies, surveys or statistical data on social and economic development. The most important informational tools are:

- the comprehensive statistical survey, the *Statistical Yearbook of the Dubai Emirate;*
- statistical books and bulletins;
- the economic survey for private sector; and
- all types of plots used in the survey.

Possible investment opportunities in the business sector

- Preparing legal studies for issues related to practising commercial activity and consulting thereon.
- Engineering and architectural studies and related services such as aviation engineering, communications, electronic and technological engineering.
- Technical consultancy, undertaking studies and providing services in the agricultural and oil industries.
- Administrative and economic studies such as marketing research, advertising, computer consultancy, transport, feasibility studies for new projects and managerial training.

Procedure for licensing commercial projects

The procedure for licensing commercial projects is as follows:

1. Select the legal status suitable to the commercial project, which shall be determined in accordance with the type of the business activity to be practised, the amount of capital to be invested and other considerations.
2. Obtain a special approval in case of activities that require such approvals from the concerned authorities. If the activity is just to practise an ordinary trading activity, the applicant may start directly with step 3.
3. Obtain a trade licence from the Department of Economic Development.
4. Register the firm with the Dubai Chamber of Commerce and Industry.

The community services sector

The community services sector includes:

- educational services;
- medical treatment and social welfare services; and
- community and other personal services.

As a result of the changes that took place in business activities many old industries, professions and crafts vanished. In the meantime, these changes created a wide economic base in all areas of activity, many of which did not previously exist. As the technical and professional expertise required for development processes could not be achieved in a limited period of time, there was a need to have professional firms specialized in offering such modern services; these firms would be able to cope with the scientific and technical development by means of their technical staff and previous technological expertise. As a result, today there are many firms operating in investment in the community services sector.

Educational services

The government has not monopolized offering educational services through its organizations, schools and institutes. The opportunity has been given to those interested in this field to set up private firms specialized in offering educational services as an auxiliary to the government educational institutes. Furthermore, the existence of foreign communities requires private schools to teach the children of these communities by adapting suitable syllabi. Therefore, there is still an opportunity to establish educational and social welfare institutions such as kindergartens; nurseries; elementary, intermediate and secondary schools; and professional institutes teaching vocational subjects such as commercial, agricultural and industrial education. Opportunities also exist for opening fine arts institutes, film institutes, theatre and music schools, community colleges (teaching technical education for two years or more after high school), language institutes, computer training institutes and educational institutes offering private tuition and business services.

There is still a need for institutes specialized in teaching beginners secretarial services, shorthand, and typing. Others also needed include driving schools and social welfare institutes, eg for the disabled and the blind.

Medical treatment and social welfare services

Economic and social development plans have had an effect on the attention given to the public-health sector and the medical and treatment services given to citizens and expatriates. Hospitals, clinics, dispensaries and different health centres have been established. The development plans had also their indirect effects: the intermigration of manpower led to an increase in the population and exerted pressure on the government budget to meet the expenses of a good quality health service because of the precautionary measures needed to be taken to curb more incoming infections.

The manpower influx from other nations has also led to an increase in the activity of some subsidiary sectors such as pharmacies selling medicines, chemicals and pharmaceutical products; laboratories that perform diagnostic examinations and medical analysis; dental laboratories; naturopathy institutes; medical and treatment consultancy offices; and clinics providing specialized services for different conditions. The activity of these clinics is restricted to contacting specialized hospitals and surgical clinics and medical centres abroad.

Community and other personal services

Two decades ago cultural activities were confined to those practised by government schools and institutes and some public clubs and institutions. Sports activities were limited to certain clubs; football was the only game practised. However, the modernization efforts that the government endeavoured to implement in accordance with the designed plans covered all aspects of life: in addition to the cultural services provided by government institutions, the private sector is also rendering specialized services such as film and television production, as well as broadcasting serials, documentaries and television programmes for educational purposes. These services exist alongside firms that buy retransmission rights by using television closed circuits and other educational services.

Recreational services are also available through specialized institutions, such as clubs that have the facilities to engage in rowing, sailing, speed-boat racing, tennis, car racing and bowling. Also on offer are public gardens, folklore troupes and facilities (such as halls, rings and playgrounds) that provide recreational means. There are also organizations that provide special services such as planning wedding parties, displaying and training folklore arts, designing wedding stands, organizing music and singing bands as well as photographing weddings and celebrations.

Possible investment opportunities

The investment areas in this sector are numerous, most of which exist because of a lack of firms currently offering specialized services, existing services being unable to meet increasing needs, or for these firms to offer services of a high standard. Some of these investment opportunities include the following:

- educational services through schools, institutes and higher colleges of technology;
- medical and treatment services through specialized clinics, hospitals and related services;
- production of films, television and broadcasting programmes, documentaries and audiovisual means for educational purposes;
- recreational centres equipped with various sports facilities;
- other personal services such as hairdressing and beauty salons, fashion design and tailoring among others.

Licensing procedure for firms in the community services sector

The licensing procedure consists of the following steps:

1. Select a suitable legal form, which is determined in accordance with the activity to be practised, the size of the invested capital and other important factors.
2. Obtain special approval from the relevant authorities in the case of activities that require such. If the activity does not require such approval, the applicant may proceed directly with step 3.
3. Complete the licensing procedure with the Department of Economic Development.
4. Register the firm with the Dubai Chamber of Commerce and Industry.

Free Zones and Industrial Cities

3.5

The Dubai Port Authority and Jebel Ali Free Zone

Data Management and Business Research Department, DCCI

Dubai Ports, Customs and Free Zone Corporation (DPCFC)

The DPCFC was established according to the law issued by the late HH Sheikh Maktoum bin Rashid Al Maktoum, former Vice-President and Prime Minister of the UAE and ruler of Dubai. The law stated that the corporation should have a body corporal, a financial and administrative independent entity, and be managed on a commercial basis. According to the new law, the establishment includes the Dubai Ports Authority (DPA), Dubai Customs Department (DCD) and the Jebel Ali Free Zone Authority (JAFZA); companies affiliated to each authority shall be attached to the corporation.

The DPCFC supervises the tasks of DCD as well as DPA and attached companies, in particular supervising, controlling and coordinating tasks of affiliated bodies. Other duties include laying down plans and working programmes of the DPCFC and preparing the draft budget and that of other bodies.

The merger of these three departments has contributed to a better service for the public, as it has enabled the exchange of expertise, particularly in the areas of management, marketing and technology. The merger also means that clients now deal with only one authority instead of three. This fits in well with a worldwide drive to create stronger economic entities that are more capable of coping with current and future challenges.

DPA

On a world scale, the DPA is extremely competitive while offering facilities comparable to the best international ports. It was also named best seaport in the Middle East for the seventh consecutive year in 2001 and best container terminal operator in the region. Since its official launch in October 2000, the MyDPA portal (www.MyDPA.co.ae) has received an overwhelming response from customers. One of the many benefits associated with MyDPA is that manifest processing has been reduced from one hour to immediate. Currently 95 per cent of DPA customers are using the services of the MyDPA portal.

The new 'smart rail' system, based on a digital global positioning system (DGPS), has been introduced to facilitate the operation of the rubber-tyred gantry cranes (RTGs) currently in use in the terminal, and to ensure that container positioning within the yard can be effectively accessed automatically and immediately. The leading technology also facilitates the automatic steering of the RTGs as they traverse the yard en route to their next location. The DPCFC has successfully connected its internal systems of the companies resources department, Maximo, which has been developed in cooperation with Tejari.com to achieve the electronic commercial B2B exchange between companies through the internet.

This success is obvious evidence of the benefits that establishments can achieve from Tejari.com, which provides effective interfacing between the various stages of electronic trade exchange. For DPA, this link enables it to coordinate its purchase cycle and procure the necessary machinery instantly through the network, thus eliminating several bureaucratic procedures and accelerating cargo delivery and maintenance services.

DCD

DCD organizes open training courses for representatives of private companies to orient them to the new services. Over 1,500 representatives have attended these courses. On demonstration of its total commitment to the Dubai government's drive toward e-governance, DCD has recently introduced e-Mirsal, an electronic data exchange service that saves considerable time and effort for importers and exporters and helps create a paperless environment. Developed in-house by DCD's UAE staff, e-Mirsal offers a host of benefits for both the organization itself and its clients. It:

- enables clients to process their custom clearance transactions without the need for personally appearing before customs centres;
- requires no technical support;
- is easy to use;
- enables clients to pay charges through electronic customs accounts thanks to its highly effective security system;
- enables online registration and enquiry; and
- enables online processing of customs-related documents (import, export, re-export, duty-free zones) and online appointment of customs clearance agents.

Several services will be added to this programme in the near future to be linked with most of the competent government, federal and local institutions and departments to carry out all commercial transactions. This programme will also render electronic registration for the digital codes with the department pertinent to the company's clearance of transaction and to carry out the different customs data such as import and export, re-export, data on the free zones, sending of the electronic authorization by the concerned organizations to the clearance companies, and to allow customs agents using importers' accounts in carrying out electronic transactions.

In order to enhance Dubai's commercial position as a centre of import and re-export, DCD – which is a part of the Dubai Ports and Free Zones – established the Dubai Customs Automobile Zone (Ducamz). Consi-dered the largest of its kind worldwide, Ducamz (located over an area of eight million square feet in the Ras Al Khor area) started commercial activity in 1999, predominantly by supplying Asian markets with right-hand-drive cars. Ducamz has offices attached to DCD and Jebel Ali Free Zone as well as government corporations in Dubai and insu-rance offices to finalize its motor transactions. Ducamz has also over 371 showrooms.

Jebel Ali Free Zone

Since its establishment in February 1985, Jebel Ali Free Zone has been able to attract national and multinational companies and contributed to placing the name of the UAE, and Dubai in particular, on the world commercial map.

Jebel Ali Port, within the free zone, is the largest man-made port in the world. It is a modern and efficient hub, with a capacity to handle even the largest container ships, car carriers, ro-ro vessels, bulk carriers and general and specialized cargo vessels. Goods reaching Dubai are speedily discharged at the DPA terminals at Jebel Ali or Port Rashid in Dubai City. Both ports receive more than 125 cargo lines from Asian, African and European countries among others.

JAFZA offers unique benefits for investors such as:

- being an open market to other international markets;
- 100 per cent foreign ownership;
- no personal income and corporate taxes for 50 years, a concession that is renewable;
- 100 per cent repatriation of capital profits;
- modern efficient communications;
- no recruitment problems;
- in-house e-business support (MyJAFZA portal service);
- no restrictions on currency and exchange;
- excellent support services from container terminals at the port;
- unique staff accommodation and modern community housing;
- on-site branches for the chamber of commerce, international banks, insurance firms and consultancy offices; and
- owners of premises for land lease can be mortgaged for bank facilities.

The reasons for the success of the Jebel Ali Free Zone are not hard to understand when you look at its distinguished geographic location. No major markets in the Middle East are more than a 24-hour drive away, all major ports in the region are within 48 hours' sailing distance. Europe is 14 days away, Japan 20 days and South Africa 9 days. Additionally, setting up a company in Jebel Ali Free Zone does not require a local partner. Therefore, companies retain 100 per cent control of their business at all times. No import and export duties are applied within the free zone and all profits can be transferred out of the country as and when required.

Since the establishment of the Jebel Ali Free Zone and until 1990, the number of companies based there was not more than 200. There are now, however, more than 2,350 companies from more than 100 countries all over the world. The zone was the first free zone in the world to receive ISO 9000 in 1998 and ISO 9001 in 2000. Unlike the industries in most of the free zones around the world, where the industrial investment percentage is about 3–4 per cent, industrial projects here reached 25 per cent of the total number of projects based in the free zone. All this was achieved due to the strong infrastructure and the presence of the vast lands that suit the set-up of such projects. The commercial activities of companies based in the free zone differ; these industries include those focused on wood, furniture, paper, printing, publishing, textiles, ready-made clothes, foodstuffs, beverages, chemicals, petroleum, coal, plastic and metal among others.

The nationality of companies in the Jebel Ali Free Zone varies: Arab companies (including those from the UAE) represent 27 per cent, European companies 25 per cent, those affiliated to the Indian Peninsula 25 per cent, American companies form 7 per cent, Far Eastern companies 8 per cent while companies from other parts of the world form 8 per cent.

Making use of computer capability advantages, JAFZA was able to achieve the best customer satisfaction, which in turn will improve current and future business. MyJAFZA, the e-business portal introduced in October 2001, is considered the best tool to improve the entire JAFZA business processes and services. The services provided by JAFZA include the processing of tourist visas, work visas, visa renewals, health cards, company licences and the renewal of company contracts. These services represent more than 60 per cent of free services provided by administration affairs in Jebel Ali Free Zone.

Mohammed bin Rashid Technology Park (MRTP)

MRTP was announced by the Executive Chairman of the DPCFC in May 2002 as an independent new project under the umbrella of the Corporation. An initial area of 3 square kilometres was allocated to the project. The objective of this important project is to enhance a knowledge-based economy by providing a regional platform and hub for the transfer, acceleration and indigenization of technology. MRTP is also a platform for the promotion and commercialization of innovation.

The activities of the companies in the park will include:

- research and development;
- laboratories;
- training in fields related to MRTP;
- innovation incubation;
- design and engineering and support services;

- process development and technology upgrading;
- technology transfer and indigenization;
- prototype development and spin-offs;
- hi-tech manufacturing;
- logistic centre for hi-tech parts; and
- investment in hi-tech fields.

MRTP is concentrating on certain demand-driven and resource-driven clusters but also internationally linked hi-tech fields including:

- desalination and water resources;
- environmental and waste management;
- oil and gas and petrochemicals;
- clean energy, such as solar and wind energy;
- materials sciences;
- agrotechnology;
- biotechnology and pharmaceuticals; and
- other hi-tech fields.

3.6

Free Zones in Dubai

Data Management and Business Research Department, DCCI

Dubai Technology and Media Free Zone

The Dubai Technology and Media Free Zone is a tax-free commercial site set up by the Dubai government to support the development of knowledge-based industries. The free zone has three separate industrial clusters – one for the ICT sector, another for the media industry and a third for diverse companies that create and disseminate knowledge including education and training institutions.

The free zone offers significant business incentives to assist growth and reduce the costs of opening or relocating a business. Companies in the free zone have 100 per cent ownership of their businesses and pay no taxes on sales, company earnings and private income. Businesses can obtain land on 50-year leases to set up their own facilities. The free zone also offers 100 per cent repatriation of capital and profits, no currency restrictions, effortless registration and licensing, stringent cyber regulations and protection of intellectual property. There is a single window for applying for all government approvals and services, including those pertaining to trade licences, visas and work permits.

Dubai Internet City

Dubai Internet City (DIC) is a strategic base for ICT companies targeting emerging markets in a vast region extending from the Middle East to the Indian subcontinent, from Africa to the CIS countries, covering 1.6 billion people with a GDP of US$1.1 trillion. Within a short space of time a dynamic international community of ICT companies has established itself in DIC. The global ICT giants are all here: Microsoft, Oracle, HP, IBM, Compaq, Dell, Siemens, Canon, Logica, Sony Ericsson and Cisco, to name just a few.

The cluster of ICT companies in DIC comprises software development, business services, web-based and e-commerce, consultancy, sales and marketing and back-office operations. DIC provides a scalable state-of-the-art technology platform for companies looking to provide cost-effective business process outsourcing (BPO) services such as call-centre operations.

DIC provides an environment that attracts each and every element of the value chain for an ICT business. In addition, it has developed programmes that can be leveraged by the ICT community to explore and expand channel development opportunities. The burgeoning ICT cluster at DIC also offers a high standard of business interaction and networking opportunities that can be utilized for enhanced problem solving and knowledge sharing.

Application procedure for DIC

Individuals or entities interested in being part of the DIC business community are required to fill out an application form, which can either be downloaded from the DIC website (www.dubaiinternetcity.com) or obtained from its sales department (Tel: +971 4 3911111, Fax: +971 4 3968777).

Dubai Media City

Dubai Media City was inaugurated in January 2001. Strategically located in Dubai at the crossroads of the Middle East, Africa and South Asia, Dubai Media City is rapidly emerging as a global media hub. The City provides an advanced infrastructure and supportive environment for media-related businesses to operate globally out of Dubai.

Dubai Media City is the place where every kind of media business – specifically broadcasting, publishing, advertising, public relations, research, music, new media and production and post-production – can thrive. The facility offers an environment that allows companies and individuals to operate with collective synergy and individual freedom.

Dubai Media City is expanding its infrastructure to provide more space for a richer and more diverse community of media companies. It is building commercial, residential, educational, medical and recreational facilities to enhance its range of services together with the quality of life of the members of its community.

Application procedure for Dubai Media City

Individuals or entities interested in being part of Dubai Media City are required to fill out an application form, which can either be downloaded from the Dubai Media City website (www.dubaimediacity.com) or obtained from its sales department (Tel: +971 4 3914555, Fax: +971 4 3914616).

Knowledge Village

Knowledge Village, the Dubai Technology and Media Free Zone's knowledge-focused initiative, aims to create the infrastructure and environment for a variety of organizations and individuals to create and disseminate knowledge. Knowledge Village seeks to provide the right conditions for the development of scholarship, education, training, ideas, creativity, innovation and entrepreneurial expertise. It offers a campus ambience with creatively stimulating and welcoming spaces for students, professionals, teachers, instructors, researchers and scientists to interact formally and informally.

A wide range of organizations will find Knowledge Village the ideal base for their operations. These include: e-learning companies, educational institutions, research and development organizations, corporate training institutions, innovation organizations, science and technology institutes, certification and testing organizations and incubators.

Dubai Airport Free Zone

The Dubai Airport Free Zone Authority (DAFZA) was established in 1996, but it only became fully operational in 1999 when the construction of its facilities was completed. The following year, DAFZA became a fully independent authority. The idea behind its establishment was to create an ideal business environment for large, international companies that select the zone not only as a base for UAE activities but as regional base for manufacturing, distribution and services.

Since DAFZA is situated within the vicinity of an airport, activities permitted at the zone are limited to high-value, low-volume products that require a rapid access to markets. Therefore, DAFZA is as ideal location for hi-tech/IT products, luxury items, jewellery, light industry/assemble operations and activities related to the aviation industry. DAFZA has already attracted 141 companies, many of which are high-calibre international blue-chip companies selected from more than 400 applicants.

The Dubai Airport Free Zone provides attractive business incentives for investors:

- 100 per cent foreign ownership;

- a corporate tax holiday for 15 years renewable for an additional 15 years;
- no personal income tax;
- freedom to repatriate both capital and profits;
- full exemption of import duties;
- no currency restrictions;
- an ideal business location and over 1.5 billion people in the Asian and CIS markets;
- located just 15 minutes from Port Rashid and only 5 minutes from the city centre, reducing response times and transportation costs;
- office-window operation for a wide ranges of services;
- companies are sponsored in their dealings with local government agencies such as sponsoring companies' personnel and handling all the related employee residency products;
- all cargo handling, storage and distribution needs are met efficiently with 'just-in-time' delivery systems through superior logistics services;
- there is a world-class infrastructure, which includes digital communications, satellite facilities, reliable power supply and ultramodern equipment and utilities.

The first construction phase of DAFZA was completed in January 1999 and included two four-storey buildings totaling 9,500 square metres, 24 warehouse units, each covering 353 square metres and 27,000 square metres of undeveloped plot allocated for companies to construct their own premises. DAFZA has successfully rented 100 per cent of its current building and warehouses and the second phase expansion of the new building has been successfully completed. The expansion includes a total office space of 10,830 square metres in the new building of which 41 per cent is already reserved and 14 warehouse units tailored to meet customers' needs. Also, DAFZA has already proceeded with phase three of the expansion to cope with increased demand.

Application procedure for Dubai Airport Free Zone

Individuals or entities in interested in being part of the Dubai Airport Free Zone are required to fill out an application form, which can either be downloaded from the Dubai Airport Free Zone website (www.dafza.gov.ae), or obtained from its sales department (Tel: +971 4 2995555, Fax: +971 4 2995500).

Dubai Metals and Commodities Centre (DMCC)

The inauguration of DMCC and the announced plan to build three gold refineries in Dubai come under a new initiative by HH Sheikh Mohammed bin Rashid Al Maktoum, Dubai Crown Prince and UAE Minister of Defence. In the next few years, this initiative will see Dubai cater for as much as half the world's gold, now ranging between 2,300 and 2,400 tonnes per year.

DMCC is a new centre that provides a full range of facilities for trading in gold, diamonds and key commodities. It is a free zone offering 100 per cent ownership and a 50-year tax holiday to resident companies. The facility will offer a full service to those organizations involved in gold trading with physical trading facilities, storage, hallmarking/assaying as well as package and delivery facilities available on-site. Three refineries will also be housed within the complex. Trading facilities, a convention centre, a training centre and a gems lab will be available to DMCC resident companies in the diamond trade while the commodities industry will be provided with world-class trading, storage and logistics facilities.

DMCC will provide a superb proposition for global players in the gold, diamond and commodity businesses. A strategic location, world-class facilities and a secure, regulated environment will all be available to companies based at DMCC. The physical location of Dubai City is a huge asset in this project as it is close to many of the key markets. Another huge asset is the opportunity to build on the established infrastructure that we have in place particularly in the gold trade.

Regulatory framework

The DMCC will have an advisory board whose responsibilities will be to agree the strategic priorities for the centre and which will also be tasked with managing plans for its development. There will also be specific, individual management committees for gold, diamonds and commodities. The regulatory framework is currently being developed but transparency and flexibility are key objectives in establishing a regulatory environment that is of international standards.

Strategic partners for resident companies in the gold industry will include banks, refineries, jewellery/coin dealers and central banks. Those from the diamond industry will be partnering with banks and jewellery dealers as well as other international centres, while commodities organizations will work with trading companies and international exchanges.

The DMCC will have the broadest possible geographical reach working with organizations and companies throughout Asia, Africa, Europe, the USA, South America and Australia. The centre will deal with three basic commodities: sugar, tea and aluminum.

DMCC advantages

Advantages of the DMCC include a superior infrastructure and logistics set-up, a politically stable environment and proximity to the world's major gold markets (particularly India) – all these give Dubai a clear edge over the rest of the world. Additionally, aside from the strategic location, the project itself offers unparalleled advantages: 100 per cent ownership (being in a free zone), tax holiday for up to 50 years, application of international standards, world-class logistics, security and safety.

Investment potentials

With the support of Dubai as a key player in international trade, this project is poised to attract top-notch business personnel and investors from all parts of the world. This will reflect positively on the national economy. While gold-related activities will involve trading, manufacture and storage, diamond-related activities will be confined to trading only. Dubai's international image as a quality-conscious environment is another reason why the project should have high stakes for success.

The new initiative aims at consolidating Dubai's international standing and contributing to the enhancement of gold output and the flow of the yellow metal through Dubai's distinguished market.

Dubai International Finance Centre (DIFC)

The driving force behind Dubai's success is the government's vision and strategy for economic development. Although a leader in technology and infrastructure, Dubai is building its international financial centre on the simple truth that it is people that create wealth in an environment of stability and openness. Dubai will build the DIFC on four firm foundations:

- *World-class regulation and transparency*. A global finance centre of the 21st century has to be open and well regulated so that it is trusted by other jurisdictions and companies who locate in it, knowing their reputation is safe.

- *The creation of new financial capital markets.* These new markets will help bring prosperity to the entire region. Financial capital moves to where it is safest and best rewarded, so DIFC's combination of total transparency and zero tax enables Dubai to benefit from the global flight to quality.
- *A great environment for people.* DIFC's work environment is highly efficient for financial institutions, corporations and professional service firms. Its leisure environment is world class – from great beaches and the world's first seven-star hotel to famous racing, golf and cricket events.
- *An oasis of stability.* DIFC operates in a political environment that is stable, an economic environment of sustainable growth and a social environment that is safe and pleasant – with a near-zero crime rate.

Situated as a bridge between the financial centres of Europe and Asia, DIFC is a platform for accessing the trillion-dollar regional market. It is a gateway for the flow of capital between the region and international capital markets. For more information about DIFC please visit its website: www.difc.ae.

3.7

Dubai's Infrastructure

Data Management and Business Research Department, DCCI

Introduction

The government of Dubai has devoted the majority of its attention to setting up the infrastructure, which is one of the most important prerequisites for economic and social development. During the 1970s huge funds were invested into infrastructural facilities, which were completed in the same decade; as a result, Dubai today yields the optimum return on investment. The most important facilities are as follows:

- airports;
- seaports;
- ship repairing and marine engineering services;
- internal roads and highways;
- telecommunications;
- water and electricity;
- postal services; and
- international trade exhibitions.

Airports

Dubai Department of Civil Aviation

Civil aviation traffic in Dubai started in 1937 when the first seaplane belonging to Imperial Airlines landed in the Dubai Creek. The real start of civil aviation in Dubai, however, goes back to 1938 when British aircraft used to fly to Dubai airport three times a week. At this time the airport was simply a modest runway prepared for the landing of small propeller aircraft.

The second stage of civil aviation, needed by the exigencies to develop the emirate of Dubai, was marked by the construction of a small international airport 4km away from the city and providing it with necessary equipment; this took place in 1959. Aviation traffic developed rapidly and the establishment of the Dubai Department of Civil Aviation in March 1971 reflected the speedy development achieved by Dubai in respect of its infrastructure. It also gave a real indication of the distinguished location of Dubai on the map of the modern aviation world and was able to cope with civil aviation traffic that grew at high rates in conjunction with the increasing importance of Dubai as a centre for local and regional trade.

Dubai International Airport

Dubai International Airport is considered the Middle East's premier and busiest airport. In 2003, despite the impact of global events, it registered a 15 per cent growth in passengers' throughput, which totaled 17 million. Dubai's liberal 'open skies' policy has attracted a large number of the world's international airlines. Many fly dedicated services into and out of the emirate, while others use Dubai as a major transit stop on their intercontinental routes. The number of scheduled international airlines using Dubai International Airport is more than 100, providing passengers with a choice of 140 destinations.

Anticipating the travel demands of the 21st century, the Dubai Department of Civil Aviation commenced a US$540 million expansion programme in 1997, which was designed to turn Dubai International Airport into an even more user-friendly and efficient airport and maintain the emirate's position as the aviation and business hub of the region. The expansion programme culminated in the new state-of-the-art Sheikh Rashid Terminal, which opened in April 2000. Architecturally, its design is unique – an aerodynamic steel structure with glazed panels in a blue-green tint, making it a tourist attraction in itself.

The five levels of Sheikh Rashid Terminal incorporate a 100-room five-star hotel offering high-quality accommodation and restaurants, as well as a fully equipped business and conference centre. It also includes a boarding level with 27 contact gates, 47 passenger loading bridges and spacious holding lounges for passengers.

Forecasts predict that 30 million passengers will pass through Dubai International Airport by 2010; keeping this in mind, the Dubai Department of Civil Aviation announced the US$2.5 billion second phase of expansion developed in November 2001. The second phase will include the construction of Terminal 3, Concourse 2, Concourse 3 – all of which will be exclusively for Emirates Airlines – and a 'cargo megaterminal'. The construction work began in early 2002 and should finish by the end of 2006. This expansion will raise the capacity of Dubai Airport from 25 million passengers to 60 million passengers. Table 3.7.1 shows the development of aircraft traffic at the airport during 2002 and 2003.

Table 3.7.1. Airport traffic during 2002 and 2003

Airport	2002	2003
Scheduled flights	123,193	141,766
Non-scheduled flights	20,533	21,292
Arriving passengers (discharged)	7,522,283	8,651,712
Departing passengers (uplifted)	7,376,965	8,523,354
Transit	1,074,143	887,278
Arriving cargo (tonnes)	425,405	505,336
Departing cargo (tonnes)	338,788	423,422

Source: Department of Civil Aviation, Dubai

Duty-free complex

Dubai's duty-free shopping complex is located at the Rashid Terminal occupying 5,400 square metres. It is recognized as one of the most distinguished duty-free facilities in the world. The aim of setting up and continued renovation of this complex is to consolidate the role of Dubai as a regional trade centre. As an international shopping centre, the complex is continuously securing its position in the Middle East region, while the duty-free facilities are keeping pace with the tremendous developments that have taken place in air facilities and services in Dubai.

Cargo Village

The new air-cargo complex, Cargo Village, opened for business in the summer of 1991. This project was established as a result of the steady increase in the rates of air and sea cargo and to facilitate transshipment operations between the Indian subcontinent, Southeast Asia, the Far East and European countries. Many important considerations were taken into account when designing this village to make it an integrated complex meeting present and future requirements of various kinds of cargo, unloading and storage activities. It was designed to accommodate the increase of the cargo rates expected during the next few years and to provide adequate space for future expansions.

At present Dubai Cargo Village can handle up to 928,758 tonnes of cargo per annum. Due to continuous growth in cargo handling, plans are under way to implement the first stage of the 'cargo megaterminal', which will eventually have the capacity to handle 3 million tonnes of freight. The main components of the project include the hall 'B' express mail centre, the 'cargo megaterminal', administrative and agents facilities, a multistorey car park, elevated roadway, central unity plant, mosque and flower centre.

Seaports

The importance of Dubai ports is based on the strategic location of the emirate, which has qualified these parts to play an essential role in receiving the commercial vessels coming from the ports of the Arabian Gulf region, Indian subcontinent and East Africa for hundreds of years. Today, Dubai ports are considered the most important facilities of the emirate's infrastructure in terms of their contribution to creating the most suitable business environment. They have also made Dubai a regional distribution hub for transit trade between the East and West.

Dubai ports are considered the most successful among the Gulf ports in terms of coping with the rapid growth and development of sea transport industry. During the last decade, they started to introduce new methods of loading and unloading container vessels that require special equipment. The major development in sea transport, particularly by the container vessels, had a direct effect on all land and air transport operations.

Means of transport revenues have become a source of large revenue. The great change in sea-, land- and air-transport operations was made by introducing container transport and designing the vessels under specifications to suit this type of transportation; Dubai has developed its ports and marine facilities to cope with this type of transportation.

Port Rashid and Jebel Ali Ports

In 1969 the late Sheikh Rashid bin Saeed Al Maktoum issued his instructions for a four-berth deep-water harbour to be constructed near to the mouth of Dubai Creek, with the foresight that it could be easily increased. Even before the four berths were completed, a further 11 berths were added.

Rashid Port was completed in 1972. The port's location near to the city centre, its all-new infrastructure and Dubai's thriving business community made it an instant success. By 1978 the number of berths was increased to 35 – including five berths that were large and deep enough to handle the largest container vessels. This attracted a growing number of main shipping lines to Dubai, as it was the dynamic redistribution and transshipment hub of the Middle East. In 1976, the late Sheikh Rashid gave instructions for an even more ambitious project: the construction of the world's largest man-made harbour at Jebel Ali. This was completed in 1979.

Although complementing Port Rashid in terms of trade and transshipments, the concept of Jebel Ali was geared more towards industrial development and soon attracted major aluminium, gas and cement projects. Establishing the Jebel Ali Free Zone around the port made the location a magnet for international business looking for the best facilities, competitively priced overheads and the freedom to operate with an offshore status.

Jebel Ali Port and Free Zone already shared the same management, and their merger with Port Rashid in May 1991 led to a dramatic increase in throughput. For the first time, the combined ports handled over 1 million 20-foot equivalent units (TEUs). Jebel Ali's container traffic soared over 50 per cent and Port Rashid's increased by a further 10 per cent to total 1.22 million TEUs. This established Dubai Ports Authority (DPA) as the sixteenth busiest container harbour in the world. Growth continued throughout the 1990s and over the years DPA handled over 4.19 million TEUs. The Jebel Ali Free Zone hosts more than 2,400 companies from over 100 countries.

Exports and re-exports from Dubai and particularly from Jebel Ali Free Zone are on the rise. DPA has frequently demonstrated its ability to adapt quickly to changing trade patterns by picking up considerable business such as the re-export of base and non-ferrous metals.

DPA is one of the leading transshipment centres in the world, serving more than 125 shipping lines. It is ranked among the leading container ports of the world and in 2003 increased its container traffic to 5.1 million TEUs, representing growth of 22.8 per cent over 2002. Between them, the twin terminals of Jebel Ali and Port Rashid handled 13,232 vessels in 2003, including 5,124 container vessels.

Dubai Creek

For a long time, Dubai Creek was an important trading position for Dubai and the countries of the region where it formed an important and safe harbour for the sailing ships and dhows visiting from the Arabian Gulf, the Indian subcontinent and East African ports. Those ships used to be loaded with various cargo, either for local distribution or re-export.

About three decades ago, Dubai Creek was only a watercourse where boats encountered some obstructions and shallow spots that hindered commercial ships entering or sailing through. It was very difficult for ships to enter the creek channel because of the current flow, which also made loading and unloading operations very exhausting and time-consuming. Nevertheless, being the only port or harbour, Dubai Creek was an important element in establishing the commercial position of the emirate.

The importance of Dubai Creek as a site for high rates of commercial activity in Dubai was a justification to introduce some necessary improvements in order to receive large vessels, facilitate loading and unloading activities and make it suitable to handle commercial operations. This led, at the beginning of 1955, to a plan to develop Dubai Creek that involved the dredging of shallow areas, building of breakwaters and developing its beach to become a quay suitable for cargo loading and unloading thereby minimizing the time spent engaged in these operations. One side of Dubai Creek was allocated to set up a dhow harbour.

Hamriyah Port

The rise in the rate of commercial activity in Dubai in the early 1970s put great pressure on Dubai Creek, which made the government of Dubai consider the possibility of setting up another port in order to handle small fishing ships and to accommodate part of the incoming commercial ships. It was decided at that time to set up Hamriyah Port, which was very soon expanded under a contract worth AED20 million that was signed in 1975. Thus, Hamriyah Port has become one of the small ports on the Gulf coasts, prepared to receive medium-sized ships and dhows coming from different areas in the Arabian Gulf, the Indian subcontinent and East Africa.

Hamriyah Port provides many facilities, for example, wooden ships are encouraged to visit the port by being exempt from all fees. This is closely linked with the active commercial history of Dubai. The port is also equipped with all machines and tools necessary to facilitate ship handling.

Ship repairing and marine engineering services

Dubai dry docks

Dubai dry docks is a modern ship repair yard, covering a total area of 200 hectares. The yard is the largest between Europe and the Far East and includes three large graving docks and a floating dock that was constructed in-house. The yard is capable of handling the largest vessels afloat and many of the world's very large crude carriers (VLCCs) carry out their regular repair here.

Dubai dry docks has a reputation for efficiency and holds an exemplary track record on quality and timely delivery. The yard makes a substantial impact on the local economy in Dubai, providing many business opportunities to suppliers and support companies in the marine industry. In addition to its core activity of ship repairs, Dubai dry docks has progressed into more sophisticated fields such as conversion work and new buildings.

Dubai's ship-docking yard

Inaugurated in 1978, Dubai's ship-docking yard (Al Jaddaf) was built to be a site for the repair and maintenance of dhows and fishing boats. However, Al Jaddaf was rapidly expanded and diversified over the years and it can now accommodate all types of vessels, from leisure crafts and small boats to cargo vessels, supply boats and oilfield-related vessels.

Al Jaddaf is fitted with two Pearlson Syncrolift Systems with a lifting capacity of 435 tonnes (11.8 tonnes per square metre). The platform is 40 metres long and 12 metres wide, in which 42 vessels of that weight can be accommodated simultaneously. The large syncrolift has a maximum load capacity of 2,520 tonnes (36 tonnes per square metre). The platform is 100 metres long and 24 metres wide; it is divided into six berths, but may be doubled to 12-berth vessels. The large syncrolift can handle any vessel capable of passing the two openings of Al Maktoum and Al Garhoud Bridges – specifically, vessels up to 26 metres wide.

Internal roads and highways

Roads have always been considered as an indicator of cultural progress and economic prosperity. Before the federal state was established, roads were vital in the transportation of materials, equipment and services. After the federation was established, these roads were and are still the main interemirates connection link.

Based on this importance, the government of Dubai built a network of modern internal roads to link the various parts of Dubai City with each other. The government also constructed a number of bridges and tunnels connected to the rest of the country and with the neighbouring Gulf countries. The length of these roads reached 657.4km. The construction cost of these roads, bridges and tunnels exceeded AED4.5 billion. These roads are provided with many essential services.

In addition to the role of these roads in the provision of travel between the emirates, they represent another crossing for foreign trade as they reach the Sultanate of Oman from the south through Hatta or Al Ain. They also stretch north along the coast reaching Qatar, Saudi Arabia, Jordan, Syria, Lebanon and Turkey.

Telecommunications

Etisalat

Etisalat, the UAE's telecommunications corporation, was established in September 1976 to assume operation, maintenance, development and provision of telecommunication services in the UAE and has, ever since, emerged as one of the leading and advanced corporations in the field at both regional and global levels. The following facts and figures may shed light on the achievements made in the telecommunications sector:

- The number of telephone lines in operation nationwide jumped from 36,000 lines in 1976 to over 1,105,380 at the end of March 2003. These figures reflect a very high coverage of telephone service, estimated at over 36 lines for every 100 persons, a rate that nudges closer to the highest global rates known in the field.
- The number of operative telephone exchanges in the country had surged from 28 in 1976 to 263 by the end of March 2003. Meanwhile, the number of countries with which the UAE maintains direct international dial services reached 268 by the end of March 2003, compared with just 36 countries in 1976. Direct international dial circuits totaled 49,384 and local dial circuits about 386,639, compared with 340 and 203 circuits respectively in 1976.
- All telephone exchanges throughout the country have been upgraded with state-of-the-art digital technology. Fibre-optic grids have made local and international dial services more effective and facilitated the exchange of data, leaving ample room for

accommodating future demand. More projects are planned for connecting the existing advanced network with regional and international marine fibre-optic projects.

Table 3.7.2. Growth of telecommunications services (2000–03)

Service	Number of lines			
	2000	2001	2002	2003
Telephone lines	390,665	407,563	430,613	459,620
Mobile phone sets	523,383	709,224	936,430	1,181,303
Pagers	63,704	48,274	36,295	30,383
Telefax lines	8,385	7,987	7,713	7,507
Telex lines	953	799	679	592
Internet subscribers	88,531	101,996	113,725	125,309

Source: Emirates Telecommunications Corporation

Etisalat also renders world-class acoustic and radio services. It has roaming agreements with over 250 mobile telephone operators in 112 countries to serve its mobile phone clients in the UAE, which boasts one of the highest rates of mobile phone use worldwide.

Furthermore, Etisalat offers wireless application protocol (WAP) services through general package radio service (GPRS). Clients can enjoy all the internet protocol facilities on the GSM network, and uninterrupted access to voice and data services. At present, Etisalat has several professional divisions such as Emirates Internet and Multi Media, Comtrust, Emirates Data Clearance Chamber, Emirates Telecommunications, Marine Services, Communication Centre, Emirates Vision and Ibtikar Card Systems.

Water and electricity

Dubai Electricity and Water Authority

Dubai Electricity and Water Authority was established on 1 January 1992, under Decree No. 1 of 1992, by merging the Dubai Electricity Company with the Dubai Water Department, which were established in 1959 and exercising their responsibilities and duties through their independent financial and administrative bodies. The decree defined the objectives of the Authority as follows:

- possession, management, operation and maintenance of the stations of power generation and water desalination plants, water well fields, power transmission lines, water distribution networks, and other company and the department's assets;
- development of water resources, including underground water production and treatment to become potable and to application of the appropriate methods for storing, transporting and distributing water to the consumers in Dubai Emirate; and
- undertaking all projects relating to electricity production and water supply to meet public demand and the requirements of economic development.

Installed power generation and water desalination capacities

Until recently, Dubai was dependent on three power stations, the oldest of which is the Diesel Plant, which was completely suspended in 1983. This station consisted of 16 diesel engines with a design capacity of 60MW, and built during the period 1961–73. At present, the Authority operates five stations with an installed production capacity of 2,976 MW:

- *Jebel Ali Power and Desalination Station (D Station).* The production capacity of this station is 1,047MW and 35 million imperial gallons per day (MIGD) of desalinated water.
- *Jebel Ali Power and Desalination Station (E Station).* The production capacity of this station is 602MW and 25MIGD of desalinated water.
- *Jebel Ali Power and Desalination Station (G Station).* The production capacity of this station is 720MW and 68MIGD of desalinated water.
- *Al Aweer Station (H Station).* The production capacity of this station is 607MW.
- *Jebel Ali Power and Desalination Station (K Station).* The production capacity of this station is 40MIGD of desalinated water.

The Authority used to operate Satwa Gas Turbine Station. This station is located near Port Rashid and was built in stages between 1974 and 1978. It consists of 16 turbines with the capacity (in summer) of 320MW but currently is out of service and kept for emergencies.

Table 3.7.3 illustrates the most important statistical features of power production and water desalination from 1999 to 2003.

Table 3.7.3. Development of electricity and water production in Dubai, 1999–2003

Year	Electricity		Water	
	Generated power (GW/h)	Number of consumers	Produced water (million gallons)	Number of consumers
1999	10,588	206,275	41,403	160,515
2000	11,262	223,505	44,495	175,182
2001	12,240	240,855	47,808	190,335
2002	13,515	248,564	51,500	196,525
2003	14,795	260,876	55,968	207,242

Source: Dubai Electricity and Water Authority

Power distribution and operating system

Electric connection and the operating system are carried out from the control centre in Mushref. The operating system is called the Supervisory Control and Data Acquisition System (SCADA), which presently controls and supervises the 132 kilovolt (kv) network and the 33kv feeder centres of the 132/33kv substations. SCADA also verifies the generation process through a computer, which ensures the economic connection of the electric load. This system achieved great success and enhanced the service standards.

The total number of consumers is 260,876, out of which there are 88,506 industrial and commercial consumers and 167,575 domestic consumers. The percentage of the electric power industrially or commercially consumed is 50 per cent, while 32 per cent is sold to domestic consumers.

Water

In 1959, the government of Dubai established Dubai Water Department; in 1992 this merged with Dubai Electricity Company to form Dubai Electricity and Water Authority. As Dubai depended largely (until the 1950s) on ground water to meet population demand, the Department was entrusted with conducting geological surveys to determine the potable water areas, well drilling, and maintain the water supply to the residential, commercial and industrial areas. With the discovery of sufficient water resources in Al Awir, 25km from Dubai where the first well was drilled in 1960, Al Awir and its neighbouring areas became the major source of potable water supply to Dubai.

During the last two decades, Dubai Water Department made great efforts to meet the emirate's water requirements to cope with Dubai's outstanding commercial, economic and social developments, the increasing demand for water and to safeguard the ground water reserve. At the beginning of 1979, the first power and desalination plant was inaugurated at Jebel Ali. The construction of this plant was a part of a long-term plan to benefit from the power available in Jebel Ali Power Station.

Dubai water resources

Dubai depends on two sources for water supplies:

- artesian water wells from the underground reserves located in Al Awir, Al Wohoosh and Al Hibab 25km from Dubai. In these locations rainwater falling on the mountains and hills adjacent to other emirates is gathered. The water of these wells is fresh, pleasant and with low salinity.
- seawater desalination units producing 168MIGD.

These sources cover Dubai's present needs of water and are distributed throughout Dubai by Dubai Electricity and Water Authority through integrated networks. The Authority built many reservoirs with different capacities at various locations in Dubai to meet water demands. Table 3.7.4 shows the production growth of potable fresh water from various sources from 1999 to 2003. In addition to this, Dubai's government exerts huge efforts to develop and provide water resources in different ways. For this purpose, it adopted a long-term plan to cope with the increasing water demand during the next two decades, which is expected to reach 305MIGD by 2006.

Table 3.7.4. The growth of production of fresh water in Dubai, 1999–2003

	1999	2000	2001	2002	2003
Total water production (million gallons)	41,403	44,495	47,808	51,500	55,968
Desalinated sea water (million gallons)	38,690	41,703	45,172	48,820	53,205

	1999	2000	2001	2002	2003
Wells water (million gallons)	2,713	2,792	2,636	2,680	2,763
Number of customers	160,515	175,182	190,335	196,525	207,242

Source: Dubai Electricity and Water Authority

Postal services

Emirates Postal Corporation (Emirates Post)

The General Postal Authority transformed into a corporation called Emirates Post in May 2001 according to the Federal Law No. (8) for 2001. This turnaround was mainly targeted at introducing state-of-the-art and high-level services that would cope with competitive commercial standards. Since its launch under the Federal Law No (8) for 2001, the corporation has been exerting tremendous efforts to develop and create innovative services, and hence it entered agreements with global postal corporations and multinational companies operating in the UAE.

Emirates Post offers a wide range of postal services such as local and international orders, pick-up and delivery service, postage paid service, parcel post account, ad by post, business reply service, express mail service, sealing permit service, insured mail service, stamp-ads, postal power and attorney, franking machine service, philatelic bureau and some other special services related to government departments.

International trade exhibitions

Dubai has emphasized its portfolio as the largest and most important centre for organizing exhibitions in the Middle East. The emirate is reputed worldwide for its various facilities including its state-of-the-art communication network, modern road network and large number of hotels and shopping malls. The Dubai World Trade Centre (DWTC) is considered the largest trade centre for organizing exhibitions in the region. Moreover, several exhibitions are held in the Dubai Chamber of Commerce and Industry (DCCI) and several hotels in the emirate. Well-equipped halls with modern audiovisual facilities in addition to all other management services are available in the Chamber, Dubai Municipality and several hotels.

DWTC

DWTC, which was inaugurated in 1979, is considered an ideal venue to hold commercial exhibitions, huge conferences and specialized seminars and lectures. It plays a key role in enhancing Dubai's position as a regional exhibition and conference centre and attracts the elite companies from across the world that manage their Middle East operations from the tower where their offices are located. The DWTC tower is an impressive 39-storey building that ranks as one of the tallest in the Arab world and one of the remarkable landmarks of Dubai.

The DWTC complex contains a hotel apartment centre that offers 492 fully furnished apartments and eight exhibition halls with hi-tech equipment and facilities. The centre – only 4km from the city centre – plays a significant role for key commercial deals in the Middle East due to the important exhibitions it hosts. During the last few years, it has enhanced Dubai's position as one of the prominent international trade centres for distinguished services. These services reflect the compatible potentials that can be offered to national and foreign firms. DWTC is run by a government firm and is a member of the World Trade Centres Association.

Airport Expo Dubai

Airport Expo Dubai is located in the southwestern corner of of the Dubai International Ariport complex, adjacent to the Royal Airwing Hangars. It offers a total floor space of more than 23,000 square metres of prime meeting space spread between two column-free halls which is complemented by an extensive outdoor exhibition area (located in a central plaza between the halls) which offers an additional 4,000 square metres of space for larger and heavier exhibits. The facility also has parking to accommodate more than 3,000 vehicles and ten coaches.

Trade fairs and exhibitions

In 2005, 70 exhibitions were expected to be held in the DWTC. These exhibitions are organized by local and foreign companies or countries and held either periodically (whether annually or once every two years) or according to requirements.

Part Four
Commercial Legislation

4.1

Business Structures in the UAE: An Overview

Russell Vickers, Trowers & Hamlins, Dubai

There are a number of business structures available within the UAE, but not all of them will be available to foreign companies. The possible structures are set out below.

Companies

Joint stock companies

There are two forms of joint stock company – private and public. Their structures are largely the same, although a private joint stock company may only offer its shares to a limited number of potential investors, whereas a public joint stock company may offer its shares to the general public. Ordinarily a public joint stock company must have a minimum of 10 shareholders.

Companies undertaking certain activities, such as insurance and banking must be registered as a public joint stock company. Under the Commercial Companies Law (Federal Law No. (8) of 1984 as amended), at least 51 per cent of the shareholding in a joint stock company must be owned by a UAE national or a company wholly-owned by UAE nationals; this means the maximum shareholding of a non-UAE partner is 49 per cent.

Limited liability company (LLC)

LLCs in Dubai are governed by the Commercial Companies Law. As with joint stock companies, under the Commercial Companies Law at least 51 per cent of the shareholding in an LLC must be owned by a UAE national or a company wholly-owned by UAE nationals, meaning the maximum shareholding for a non-UAE partner is 49 per cent.

However, profits may be divided as the shareholders (more commonly known as 'partners') may agree, subject to the requirements of each emirate. In Dubai, for instance, as a matter of policy, the minimum profit-sharing entitlement of the UAE partner is 20 per cent. Distribution of surplus assets on a winding-up of an LLC is also made according to profit-sharing ratios.

The minimum share capital of an LLC is AED150,000. Certain emirates have, as a matter of policy, set a higher minimum share capital, which in the case of Dubai is AED300,000. Shares must be paid up in full immediately prior to incorporation, ie paid into a local bank account prior to the issue of the business licence by the Dubai Department of Economic Development (DDED), the local licensing authority.

The management of the LLC is entrusted to up to five directors (called 'managers'), who each have authority to operate independently within their designated areas. The managers may, if desired, be formed into a board, which takes management decisions collectively, although certain important matters are reserved, as a matter of law, to the partners. Alternatively, a General Manager may be appointed (who may also be a director) to manage the day-to-day affairs of the LLC. The director(s) are liable towards the LLC, the shareholders and third parties for all acts of fraud, abuse of authority, any violation of the Commercial Companies Law, any violation of the LLC's Memorandum of Association and mismanagement. For instance, if the General Manager (or a director) issues a cheque on the LLC's account when there are insufficient funds to meet it, he could be liable to criminal prosecution under the UAE Penal Code.

An LLC may not commence business until it holds a certificate of commercial registration, issued by the federal UAE Ministry of Economy and Planning (MEP) and an appropriate business licence, issued by the DDED. Business licences are generally renewable annually. In Dubai, a business licence will not be issued without the applicant becoming a member of the Dubai Chamber of Commerce and Industry (DCCI).

Branch office of a foreign company

The Commercial Companies Law allows foreign companies to establish a branch office in the UAE (CCL branch). The scope of activities permitted to be undertaken by branch offices varies from emirate to emirate, although generally a broad range of commercial trading activities can be undertaken.

A foreign company that wishes to establish a CCL branch in one of the emirates must obtain the consent of the MEP before a local business licence from the government of the relevant emirate is issued. The CCL branch must also have a services arrangement with a UAE national or a locally registered company, which is wholly owned by UAE nationals. The services agent is known as the national agent. A formal National Agency Agreement is required, in which the national agent undertakes to sponsor and assist the foreign company, in return for a fee. It is not advisable for a National Agency Agreement to be signed without legal advice having been taken.

Again, commercial registration, a business licence and membership of the local Chamber of Commerce and Industry are all required.

Representative office

In Dubai, in addition to the CCL branch office, there is also provision for a representative office. These may generally only conduct representative, marketing and other promotional activities and may not trade. They require a local services agent, similar to a national agent.

Free-zone entities

There are a number of free zones in operation within Dubai and others situated in other emirates. The Jebel Ali Free Zone in Dubai is by far the largest of the UAE's free zones, containing the world's largest man-made port and is now home to more than 1,000 companies. Dubai also has a number of specialist free zones such as Dubai Internet City, Dubai Media City and Dubai Airport Free Zone. Each has its own rules and regulations, but the key advantage of establishing within a free zone is that a company can be 100 per cent owned by foreign nationals in a tax-free jurisdiction.

Depending on the free zone, there are different types of business entity available. Generally, however, if a free-zone entity wishes to distribute its products within the UAE, such goods will be regarded as having been imported and may be liable to customs duties. By way of example, Jebel Ali Free Zone permits three types of legal entity: a branch of a foreign company, a single shareholder limited liability company – known as a free-zone establishment (FZE), or a multishareholder limited liability company – known as a free-zone company (FZCO). A brief description of each legal entity is set out below, but note that these can vary from free zone to free zone.

Branch of a foreign company

There is no requirement, as would be the case in mainland Dubai, for a local services agent to be appointed. In these circumstances, the foreign company receives 100 per cent of the branch's profits, which may be repatriated without deduction.

There are no minimum capitalization requirements, although the foreign company is required to provide details of its own capitalization and good standing, together with confirmation of its financial commitment to the branch.

The foreign company retains full control over the management of the branch through its representative, who is required to be locally resident. There are, however, no requirements for this individual to be a UAE national.

The branch does not need to file audited accounts.

FZE

The concept of an FZE was introduced by Law No (9) of 1992. An FZE is a single shareholder entity, which has its own legal personality and independent financial liability limited to the amount of paid-up capital. An FZE may be incorporated by preparing its own Memorandum and Articles of Association or by adopting the Implementing Regulations (No 1/92) issued by the Jebel Ali Free Zone Authority (JAFZA), which regulate the establishment of FZEs.

FZCO

An FZCO is a multishareholder entity having its own legal personality and independent financial liability limited to the amount of paid-up capital. All shares must be of the same class and there can be a minimum of two and a maximum of five shareholders.

An FZCO may be incorporated by entering into the standard form of Memorandum and Articles of Association produced by JAFZA or by adopting the Implementing Regulations (No. 1/99) of an FZCO issued by JAFZA. As this legal entity may be owned by more than one shareholder, the shareholders may require the standard form of Memorandum and Articles of Association produced by JAFZA to be amended to more accurately reflect the shareholders' contributions and profit share, management and shareholder control and any change in partners. Further, it may be appropriate for the shareholders to enter into a Shareholders' Agreement to reflect these issues in more detail. Any variations from the standard form Memorandum and Articles of Association must be approved by JAFZA prior to signature by the shareholders, which must be carried out in the presence of JAFZA officials.

Service company

The Civil Code permits the establishment of service companies, which are in essence professional partnerships. They can be appropriate for doctors, dentists and other recognized professions. These may be 100 per cent owned by foreign nationals, but do not confer limited liability. A UAE national agent must be appointed as if it were a branch office of a foreign company. The grant of licences for service companies is discretionary.

Partnership

There are three main forms of partnership within the UAE: general partnership, simple limited partnership and partnership limited with shares. These are not very common business forms. Only UAE nationals may be partners in a general partnership, while foreign investors may only be sleeping partners with a non-managerial role in a simple general partnership. A partnership limited with shares must have UAE national partners who have unlimited liability and it can then have foreign partners whose liability is limited to the share capital they have put in. The minimum capital requirement is AED500,000.

Other forms of doing business

Some companies carry on their business operations in the UAE without formally establishing a presence in one of the emirates. This can be done through a variety of contractual arrangements.

A foreign business may decide that it does not wish to invest in establishing a local commercial entity or a branch office in the UAE if, for example, it simply intends to export goods or services to the UAE. In this situation an agent, distributor or franchisee (which must be 100 per cent UAE) can be appointed.

The Commercial Agencies Law regulates these arrangements. There are certain express requirements as to the content of any agency agreement. It is possible for UAE commercial agents to register agency agreements with the MEP and this gives rise to certain rights and obligations and a high scope of statutory protection for the agent. Prior to signing an agency agreement, it is important to understand clearly the scope of the agency, the available means of terminating the agreement and the precise effect of registration.

It is possible for a foreign principal to have more than one agent registered in the UAE, as it is possible to appoint a different agent in each emirate for the same goods or services, and a different agent for different goods and services. In practice, it is quite common to divide the UAE into two territories, being Abu Dhabi on the one hand and Dubai and the northern emirates on the other.

Considerable care is necessary in the preparation of commercial agency agreements and, in relation to registration, in order to ensure their commercial effectiveness. Unregistered commercial agencies are however not subject to the Commercial Agencies Law and, accordingly, the agent is not afforded the protections as under a registered commercial agency. An unregistered commercial agency will be dealt with a purely contractual relationship between the parties.

The foregoing overview of the business structures in the UAE is not intended to as a substitute for legal advice on specific matters. The writer does not accept any liability from the use or reliance on the information contained herein. The information above is current to March 2005.

4.2

Practical Steps and Procedures for Company Incorporation in the UAE

Helen Barrett, Trowers & Hamlins, Dubai

Licensing/registration formalities

Before conducting business in the UAE, it is necessary to comply with the laws governing business activities, such as the UAE Commercial Companies Law (CCL), and to obtain an appropriate licence issued by the licensing authority in the relevant emirate. In the emirate of Dubai, for instance, licensing and registration formalities are dealt with by the Dubai Department of Economic Development (DDED). The identity of the licensing body may, however, vary from emirate to emirate. There may also be special requirements to be fulfilled in addition to those of the local licensing authority; as an example, construction-related activities require approval of the relevant municipality.

Licences for commercial activities in the UAE broadly fall into two main categories, namely, trade or professional licences. It follows that a trade licence would be granted to a trading entity, eg a limited liability company (LLC). There are a broad range of activities covered by a professional licence, which may be obtained by a foreign company conducting professional activities or by a foreign company wishing to establish a regional centre for marketing and promoting its services, ie a representative office. A professional licence also covers the supply of goods as an incidental part of providing the services, eg vehicle parts supplied by a garage repairing cars and, for the purposes of the incidental supply of goods as part of its services, the holder of a professional licence is also permitted to import these goods. It is also possible to obtain a licence to conduct business in one of the UAE's free zones that operate through an exemption to the CCL.

In this chapter, we address the formalities for establishing the most common types of legal entities: a branch of a foreign company (federal branch) of an LLC in mainland Dubai and the incorporation of an LLC in Jebel Ali Free Zone.

Establishment of a federal branch

In order to register a federal branch in the emirate of Dubai, various forms and supporting documents are required to be submitted, in Arabic, to the DDED, the local licensing authority and the Federal Ministry of Economy and Planning (MEP, formerly known as the Ministry of Economy and Commerce). Licences are generally renewable annually.

The documentation required to be submitted to the MEP is usually more protracted than that required by the DDED, although both will include the constitutional documents of the foreign company and the National Agency Agreement, which usually must be entered into by the foreign company and a UAE national or company wholly-owned by UAE nationals.

Documents originating from outside the UAE must be fully authenticated before being submitted to the MEP or DDED. This involves notarization in the same jurisdiction as the foreign company, legalization by the foreign ministry in that jurisdiction and attestation by the nearest UAE embassy. Once these documents are received in the UAE, they must be further attested by the Ministry of Foreign Affairs and translated into Arabic by a legal translator approved by the Ministry of Justice in order to be in a form acceptable to the MEP, DDED or other licensing/government authorities.

The MEP will take approximately two to three weeks from submission of the documents to assess the application. More often that not, the MEP will request further information and/or documentation if it deems necessary. Once the application is approved, and the official fees paid, the MEP will issue a certificate of no-objection to enable the application to proceed to the next stage of processing at the DDED. The certificate is valid for a period of two months but is renewable upon payment of a further fee to the MEP. It is therefore prudent for the remaining formalities to be carried out at the DDED as swiftly as possible. The MEP has recently introduced a requirement for foreign companies establishing a federal branch in Dubai to deposit a bank guarantee of AED50,000. This is usually paid to the MEP once the licensing and registration formalities have been completed at the DDED.

The federal branch must, by this time, have taken a lease of business premises, a copy of which must be submitted to the Dubai Municipality Section at the DDED as part of the application. The application will be considered by the DDED's legal department. Once the documents are approved, the DDED's finance section will prepare an invoice for licence/registration fees. The federal branch licence will be issued automatically upon settlement of the invoice.

Once its licence is issued, the company may register with the UAE Ministry of Labour and the UAE Department of Immigration to be able to sponsor its own employees. It can also open local bank accounts and obtain communications connections.

LLC

Various application forms and supporting documents must be submitted to the DDED, which is both the competent authority for the purposes of the federal registration of the LLC and the issuing authority for the purposes of the trade licence. It is prudent for the applicant to obtain approval from the DDED to the LLC's proposed objects and name prior to preparation of the LLC's Memorandum of Association. The trade name must be derived from the name of the proposed objects of the LLC or from the name of its partners. Specific approval must be obtained for use of words, such as 'Dubai', 'Emirates', 'Middle East' or 'UAE' against an additional fee. As mentioned above, it may be necessary to obtain special approval from another government body for certain activities.

The next stage is for the legal documents to be collated and the LLC's Memorandum of Association to be prepared. Documents originating from outside the UAE must be fully authenticated (as above) before being submitted to the MEP or DDED.

The LLC's Memorandum of Association must be signed before the Dubai Court Notary Public, which means that it must be translated into Arabic. It will be necessary for the foreign partner to appoint an individual in Dubai, by virtue of a fully authenticated and translated power of attorney, to attend to the incorporation formalities including the execution of the Memorandum of Association.

The notarized Memorandum of Association and the legal documents should then be submitted to the licensing section of the DDED for their review. At this stage, it will be necessary for the LLC's share capital to be deposited in a local bank and its auditors appointed. A certificate confirming the deposit of share capital will be issued by the LLC's local bankers and a certificate confirming the appointment of local auditors will be issued by the appointed auditors. Both certificates must be submitted to the DDED in order for the application to proceed.

Thereafter, the entire application is reviewed by the DDED's legal department.

The LLC must, by this time, have taken a lease of business premises, a copy of which must be submitted to the Dubai municipality section at the DDED. If all of the documents are in order, the DDED's finance section will prepare an invoice for licence/registration fees and the licence will be issued upon settlement of the invoice.

The LLC will then be required to submit an Application for Membership to the Dubai Chamber of Commerce and Industry (DCCI). This involves the completion of an application form by the LLC's general manager and submission of copies of the incorporation documents, including the trade licence, to the DCCI for approval.

After issue of the trade licence, it may then obtain communications connections. The LLC must register with the UAE Ministry of Labour and the UAE Department of Immigration to be able to sponsor its own employees and obtain membership to the DCCI. The trade licence authorizes the LLC to carry on business in and from the relevant emirate. If it wishes to establish a physical presence in another emirate, it will require a similar trade licence from that emirate.

Incorporation at Jebel Ali Free Zone

In order to incorporate a free-zone establishment (FZE) – a single-shareholder limited liability company – or a free-zone company (FZCO) – a multishareholder limited liability company – at Jebel Ali Free Zone the appropriate Application for Licence must be submitted to Jebel Ali Free Zone Authority (JAFZA), together with a short (one-page) project summary setting out the foreign company's intentions. After examination of the application forms and project summary, JAFZA will make an initial assessment and, if accepted, a provisional approval letter will be issued.

At this stage, JAFZA will then ask for the appropriate legal documents to be submitted. Documents originating from outside of Dubai must be notarized, legalized by the foreign ministry and attested by the UAE embassy. There is no requirement for further attestation by the Ministry of Foreign Affairs in Dubai or translation into Arabic.

Provided the legal documents are in order, JAFZA will issue a letter to the applicant's local bankers informing them that the bank account may be opened in order for the appropriate share capital to be deposited. Upon receipt of such monies, the local bank will issue a certificate confirming the deposit of share capital, which must then be submitted to JAFZA. At this stage, the company will be legally incorporated and the Certificate of Formation and Share Certificate will be issued.

The FZE/FZCO must take a lease of business premises from JAFZA. Accordingly, JAFZA will prepare a proforma lease, setting out the main terms and conditions of the lease, that will need to be signed by the foreign company applicant. Thereafter, an actual lease agreement and personnel secondment agreement (PSA) (which relates to the sponsorship by JAFZA of the FZE/FZCO's employees) will be prepared by JAFZA's sales department and an invoice for registration/licensing and annual rental fees will be issued for payment. The FZE/FZCO will then be asked to sign the lease and PSA (and Memorandum and Articles of Association, if appropriate) and to pay the agreed rent and licence/registration fees. The lease and licence can then be collected.

The foregoing overview of the practical steps and procedures for company incorporation in the UAE is not intended as a substitute for legal advice on specific matters. The writer (and Trowers & Hamlins) do not accept any liability from the use or reliance on the information contained herein. The information stated above is current to August 2005.

Trowers and Hamlins
28 September 2005

4.3

UAE Labour and Employment Law

Ahlam Al Jahdhamy,[*] Trowers & Hamlins, Dubai

Labour and employment law

Employment matters in the UAE are governed by the Labour Law (Federal Law No. 8 of 1980 as amended). The Law is federal and is therefore applicable to all the seven emirates of the federation.

The government body that is primarily responsible for employment matters is the Ministry of Labour and Social Affairs (MLSA). The MLSA does not strictly enforce the Labour Law and regulations but it will seek to achieve a resolution through negotiation rather than by the imposition of penalties. All disputes relating to labour matters must first be referred to the MLSA. If the employer or employee is unhappy with the MLSA's decision and the matter cannot be settled amicably, the dispute may then be referred by the MLSA to the court.

The Labour Law applies to all employees working in the private sector in the UAE, whether they be UAE nationals or expatriates. However, there are certain categories of individuals who are exempt from the Labour Law. Those exempted are:

- government workers;
- members of the armed force, police and security units;
- domestic servants; and
- agricultural workers;

[*] Since the writing of this chapter Ahlam Al Jahdhamy has left Trowers & Hamlins, Dubai.

Employees in free zones

It should be noted that, although the Labour Law stipulates that all employees (other than those exempted above) are subject to the Labour Law, in practice, employees in the free zones, such as the Jebel Ali Free Zone, Dubai Internet City and Dubai Media City, are also subject to the rules and regulations of that specific free zone.

Personal income tax

There are no personal income taxes in the UAE.

Employment contracts

The Labour Law requires that all employees have a written contract of employment executed in duplicate, each party taking one copy. The MLSA has a standard employment contract. This employment contract is not compulsory but is widely used. The required essentials for an employment contract are the same, irrespective of the employee's position.

All contracts and all instructions and circulars issued by an employer to its employees should be in Arabic and in a language understood by the employees. English is the business language of the UAE and most employment contracts entered into are in the form of dual Arabic and English text documents.

Statutory requirements for employment contracts

The statutory requirements as to the content of a contract of employment are limited to:

- the date of the employment contract;
- the date of commencement of the employment;
- the place/location of employment;
- the wages/remuneration payable;
- a statement of the employees duties; and
- the duration of the employment contract (if a fixed-term contract).

The essential components of the Labour Law

Employment contract and duration

As mentioned above, the Labour Law requires that all employees have a written employment contract. A contract of employment may be for a fixed or indefinite term. Fixed-term employment contracts are contracts for a specified duration with specific commencement and completion dates, whereas an indefinite-term employment contract is one whereby the employee continues to work for the employer from a specific date until such time as the employment contract is terminated by either party giving prior notice.

The parties are free to set a probationary time period of up to six months regardless of whether the contract is for a fixed or indefinite term. An employee may not be appointed on a probationary basis more than once with the same employer.

Working hours

In applying the rules on the maximum number of working hours, the Labour Law makes no distinction between full-time and part-time workers. Distinctions are drawn, however, between men, women and children:

- *Male workers*. The maximum number of hours that may be worked is generally eight hours per day and 48 hours per week. In the case of commercial business or hotel and restaurant staff, a maximum working day of nine hours is permitted (maximum 54 hour week). An employee's normal hours of work are to be reduced by two hours per day during the holy month of Ramadan.
- *Female employees*. The rules on maximum hours are as for male employees. However, female employees may not generally be employed to work between the hours 10pm and 7am (with exceptions, including restaurant employees and those working in the medical services).
- *Juvenile employees*. Children under the age of 15 years may not be employed. The age of majority is 18 Hijra years (approximately 17.2 Gregorian years). Employees below the age of majority may not be employed for more than six hours daily. Juveniles may not work overtime or work on Fridays. Juveniles may not work on industrial projects at night, ie between 8pm and 6am.

The limits on hours do not apply to chairmen of boards of directors, managing directors, general managers or departmental directors who have the power to hire and dismiss staff.

An employee's hours of work must be organized so as to ensure that the employee does not work for longer than five consecutive hours. During a working day that exceeds five hours an employee is entitled to a break of at least one hour. The break is not included in the calculation of working hours.

The maximum hours of work set out above may be exceeded where the employee is required to work overtime. Overtime may not exceed a further two hours' work in any one day. In return for working overtime, a worker is entitled to his/her normal salary together with an increase of not less than 25 per cent thereof. If the overtime hours fall between the hours of 9pm and 4am, the employee is entitled to an increase of 50 per cent on his normal wage.

Friday is the normal weekly holiday. If an employee is required to work on a Friday, he/she is entitled to his/her basic wage together with an increase of 50 per cent or to be compensated with an alternative rest day, at the employer's discretion. An employee should not be employed for two consecutive Fridays except those who are engaged on a daily basis.

Wages

Employees whose employment contracts stipulate an annual or monthly salary must have their wages paid at least once every month. All other workers should be paid at least every two weeks. Wages must be paid on a working day.

The Labour Law requires that wages be paid in the currency of the UAE at the place of work. That said, it is common practice for employees to be paid by direct credit to a bank account.

The only permissible deductions from wages are as follows:

- deductions to recover a loan to an employee provided that the sum deducted from the wage is no more than 10 per cent of the employee's wage entitlement;
- any sums that a worker is legally obliged to pay (this provision envisages taxation, social security payments etc – at present none of these exist);
- contributions to a savings fund established by the employer and provided for in the employment contract;

- instalments to any social plan for payments in respect of privileges or services provided by the employer and that are sanctioned by the MLSA;
- fines imposed on the employee in accordance with the employer's disciplinary code; and
- sums that the employee is legally obliged to pay as a result of a criminal or civil judgement against him, ie should an employee become a judgement debtor, there are procedures pursuant to which the judgement creditor can apply to the court for an attachment to the employee's earnings whereby the debtor's employer deducts payments from wages under court supervision.

Minimum wage
The Labour Law makes provision for a minimum wage to be set by ministerial decision. We understand that it has been set at AED600 (US$165) per month but, to our knowledge, this has not been officially gazetted.

National holidays

Most holidays celebrated in the UAE are Islamic festivals that are calculated according to the Hijra calendar. Because the Hijra calendar is a lunar calendar, the commencement of each month depends upon the sighting of a new moon, which means in turn that the precise dates cannot be predicted very far in advance. It is only when a new month starts that the dates of any holidays that fall during that month become known. The Hijra year is approximately 13–15 days shorter than a Gregorian year, which means that Islamic festivals will fall approximately 13–15 days earlier each year in terms of the Gregorian calendar.

The Islamic festivals, which are celebrated together with the holiday entitlement under the Labour Law, are as follows:

- Eid Al Fitr (breaking of the Ramadan fast): two days;
- Eid Al Adha (Feast of Immolation): three days;
- Islamic New Year: one day;
- Prophet's Birthday: one day; and
- Miraaj Al Rasool (Prophet's ascension to Heaven): one day.

In addition there are two holidays that are fixed in terms of the Gregorian calendar:

- New Year's Day: 1 January; and
- UAE National Day: 2 December.

Vacation entitlement

The Labour Law sets out the employee's vacation entitlement. During each year of employment an employee is entitled to two days for each month employed for periods of service between six months and one year; for contracts of employment that exceed one year the entitlement is at least 30 days per year. Where the employee is employed for partial years only, the holiday entitlement is calculated pro rata. An employee cannot be obliged to split annual leave into more than two periods in each year.

An employee is entitled to his/her basic salary for periods of leave. If an employee is required to work during his/her vacation period without being allowed to carry the entitlement forward to a subsequent year, then he/she is entitled to be paid twice over.

According to the Labour Law, an employee is entitled to be paid, before taking periods of annual leave, all salary entitlement up to the end of the period of leave. In practice, this is a provision that is not always adhered to by employers. Many employers are reluctant to adhere to this provision for fear of expatriate workers not returning to the UAE.

Termination issues

The Labour Law addresses termination issues, which will vary depending on the term of the employment contract. A contract of fixed duration terminates automatically on its expiry date, whereas a contract of unfixed duration may be terminated by either the employer or employee by their giving no less than 30 days' notice.

If an employer decides to terminate a fixed-term employment contract for any reason not provided for in Article 120 of the Labour Law, then the employer is required to compensate the employee for his/her loss.

Article 120 of the Labour Law permits an employer to dismiss an employee without notice in the following circumstances:

- if the employee assumed a false identity or nationality or presented forged certificates or documents;
- if the employee was appointed on probation and the dismissal occurs during or at the end of the probation period;

- if the employee has made a mistake that results in a substantial material loss for the employer;
- if the employee has contravened instructions concerning the safety of work or the place of work;
- if the employee has failed to carry out his/her basic duties in accordance with the work contract and has continued in such dereliction;
- if he/she discloses any of the secrets of the establishment in which he/she works;
- if he/she is finally convicted of an offence against honour, honesty or public decency by a competent court;
- if, during the hours of work, he/she is found to be in a state of obvious drunkenness or under the influence of drugs;
- if, while at work, he/she commits an assault on the employer, responsible manager or one of his/her work colleagues; or
- if the employee is absent without lawful cause for more than 20 days discontinuously during one year or more than seven consecutive days.

Article 121 of the Labour Law permits an employee to leave his/her work without notice in any of the following circumstances:

- if the employer fails to fulfil his/her obligations to the employee prescribed in the contract or under the Law; or
- if, as amended by Federal Law No. 12 of 1986, an assault is committed by the employer or his/her lawful representative against the employee.

End of service benefit

An employee who has completed one year or more in continuous employment is entitled to severance pay. Any days of absence from work without pay (eg unauthorized leave) are not included in the calculation of the one-year period.

Severance pay is calculated as follows: 21 days' salary for each year during the first five years of service and 30 days' salary for each year following the initial five-year period of service. The maximum severance payment that the employer is obliged to make to an employee is two years' salary. Sums due by an employee to his/her employer may be deducted by the employer from the severance pay entitlement.

An employee who is engaged on a contract of indefinite duration and who leaves the position of employment of his/her own volition after a period of continuous service of not less than one and not more than three years is entitled to severance pay of one-third of the entitlement set out above. Such an employee is entitled to the full severance pay entitlement if the period of continuous service exceeds five years.

An employee who is engaged on a fixed-term contract and who leaves the position of employment of his/her own volition before the end of the contract period is not entitled to severance pay unless the period of continuous service exceeds five years. An employee is not entitled to severance pay in the following cases:

- if he/she is dismissed from service for any of the reasons set out in Article 120 of the Labour Law or leaves work to avoid dismissal thereunder; or
- if the employee leaves work of his/her own volition and without notice in circumstances other than those set out in Article 121 of the Labour Law (for contracts of indefinite duration) or before the employee has completed five years of continuous service (for contracts of fixed duration).

Severance pay entitlement is regarded as being, in effect, in lieu of a pension entitlement. It is unusual for employers in the UAE to establish pension schemes for the benefit of their employees. This approach is reflected in the rule that where an employee dies in service, his/her estate is entitled to severance pay calculated as if the employee had ceased to be employed at the date of death.

There are no retirement schemes in the UAE. The approach that the Labour Law takes is that severance pay is effectively a pension substitute.

Emiratization

The concept of emiratization, which is to ensure that the local population is employed to the greatest extent possible, has gathered increasing importance in the UAE. The Labour Law prescribes that MLSA approval of the employment of expatriates is generally conditional on the unavailability of qualified UAE nationals. The MLSA has issued various policies that encourage and require the employment of UAE nationals in certain jobs, such as the banking and insurance sectors. A cash fine is imposed on companies and organizations failing to achieve the required emiratization quota.

The foregoing overview of the UAE employment and labour law is not intended to substitute for legal advice on specific matters. The writer does not accept any liability from the use or reliance on the information contained herein. The information stated above is current to March 2005.

4.4

Audit, Accountancy and Taxation

KPMG

Accountancy and auditing

The accounting and auditing requirements of entities registered in the UAE are set out in the Commercial Companies Law of the UAE (Federal Law No. (8) of 1984, as amended). It is also necessary to comply with the regulations of the Economic Department in each emirate.

The Commercial Companies Law requires locally registered companies and branches of foreign companies to appoint auditors to audit their financial statements. These auditors must be registered in the Register of Accountants and Auditors in accordance with the provisions of Federal Law No (9) of 1975 concerning the regulation of the accounting and auditing professions.

All commercial organizations must obtain a trade licence, which has to be renewed annually by the Economic Department of the respective emirate. However, in the case of business entities established in a free zone, this licence is obtained from the appropriate free-zone authority. In practice, audited financial statements are required to be submitted at the time of renewing the trade licence. However, each free-trade zone has its own laws and regulations, hence the accounting and audit requirements can differ between the free zones.

Structure

No accounting standards are prescribed under the UAE Commercial Companies Law; hence most companies maintain their accounts under International Accounting Standards (IAS) or International Financial Reporting Standards (IFRS).

The annual report consists of:

- balance sheet;
- income statement;
- statement of cash flow;
- statement of changes in equity;
- explanatory notes;
- auditors report;
- director's report; and
- other relevant information.

The auditor has to ensure the following information disclosed in the financial statements is in accordance with the memorandum of incorporation of the company:

- name of the company;
- legal constitution;
- location;
- partners/shareholders and their shareholding;
- nature of business;
- authorized share capital of the company;
- paid-up share capital; and
- face value of the shares.

The measure of value must be a monetary unit of UAE dirhams and the financial statements submitted to the local authorities must be in Arabic.

Essentials

Every entity must mention its financial year in its articles. Each entity, in each financial year, must prepare the financial position, a report on the entity activities during the previous financial year and the proposed method of distribution of net profits.

Every business entity that is a limited liability company or joint stock company must allocate a minimum of 10 per cent of its net profits each year to create a non-distributable statutory reserve. Such reserve may be suspended if the reserve reaches half of the paid-up capital. However, for public joint stock companies, the amount that is in excess of one-half of the paid-up capital may be used in the distribution of dividends to the shareholders in the years that the company does not achieve sufficient net profits to reach the rate specified therefore in the company articles.

Every business entity that is a limited liability company or joint stock company shall have one or more auditors selected each year by the general assembly. If the entity has two auditors, each of them must prepare a separate report. The auditor has to present a report of the results of his/her findings to the general assembly and deliver a copy thereof to both the ministry and the competent authority.

The auditor must attend the general assembly and present his/her opinion on all matters related to his/her duties particularly with regard to the company balance sheet. He/she should present his/her report to the general assembly. The report must include the following particulars:

- whether the auditor has obtained the information he/she considers necessary for the satisfactory performance of his/her duties;
- whether the balance sheet and profit and loss account are compatible with the facts and include the mandatory requirements in accordance with the provisions of the law and the company articles, and honestly and clearly reflect the true financial position of the company;
- whether the company keeps proper books;
- whether stocktaking was conducted in accordance with applied practices;
- whether the particulars mentioned in the report of the board of directors is compatible with company books; and
- whether there are any violations to the provisions of the law or the company articles during the financial year in a manner that affects the company's activities or its financial position, indicating whether to the best of his/her knowledge such violations are still existing and the extent of the information available to him/her.

The auditor's report should be read at the general assembly. Every shareholder has the right to discuss the report and request clarification of the facts mentioned therein. The records shall be kept in such a manner as to enable any person who is qualified in accounting to clearly identify:

- the financial position of the company;
- the business transaction made during the given period of time; and
- the beginning and the sequence of each transaction.

Taxation

Prior to the establishment of the UAE in 1971, British colonial administration entered into treaties with each trucial state or sheikhdom (as the emirates were then known). Discovery of oil in 1966 catalyzed the British administration to draft rudimentary tax legislation aimed at oil revenues. Most of the seven emirates have enacted taxation legislation based on the original British legislation.

Structure

There is no federal UAE tax legislation for corporate income taxes or personal income tax. However, as mentioned above, most of the emirates have enacted their own tax legislation for corporate income tax. In general, there are very few differences between the tax laws of each emirate and none of the laws are detailed or voluminous. Any tax specifics mentioned herewith have been taken from the Dubai Income Tax Decree (as amended). Note that the official Arabic document must be consulted as the definitive law, as no 'official' English translation has been issued.

The tax decrees impose corporate income tax on the taxable income of any corporate body or branch that carries on trade or business through a permanent establishment in the emirate. A permanent establishment includes a branch, management or administrative centre, or place of business, but not an agency, unless the agency habitually concludes agreements and exercises the authority of the body corporate. *It is important to note that even though this corporate tax legislation exists, at present, taxation is enforced only on foreign oil companies and branches of foreign banks.*

Practice

Corporate income tax is not enforced on all corporate entities. Only foreign oil companies (ie companies transacting in oil or oil rights, including crude oil or other hydrocarbon materials produced in the emirate) and branches of foreign banks are subject to corporate income tax and therefore required to file annual tax returns. However, the tax legislation is theoretically applicable to all corporate entities (apart from those within the free-trade zones – see below under 'Investment incentives'), and no blanket guarantee can be given regarding an indefinite exemption of foreign entities from corporate income tax.

In most emirates the amount of tax paid by foreign oil companies is based on a rate agreed in an individual concession agreement between the ruler of the emirate and the company. These concession agreements are not disclosed to the public but, in practice, the rate ranges from 55 per cent to 85 per cent.

In theory a provisional tax declaration must be lodged with the tax authority within three months after the end of the financial year, ie by 31 March. Quarterly payments are made based on this provisional declaration and assessment on the last day of the third, sixth, ninth and twelfth months following the end of the financial year. A finalized tax return must be lodged by the end of the ninth month following the end of the financial year and the final quarterly payment is adjusted accordingly following lodgement of the finalized return. In practice, however, the collection of taxes can differ. In the case of foreign oil companies, they generally 'self assess' and then pay the tax in monthly instalments on a 'pay as you go' basis. A provisional return of income is made by 31 March of the following year and any underpayment of tax has to be made good immediately. The final tax return is due on 30 June.

Branches of foreign banks are subject to tax at a rate of 20 per cent. In Dubai, Ajman, Sharjah and Fujairah specific legislation has been enacted that sets out the lower tax rate for branches of foreign banks. In other emirates (eg Abu Dhabi) agreements between the foreign bank and the ruler of the emirate set out the tax rate. Branches of foreign banks must submit their tax returns by the end of the third month following the end of the taxable year. The tax due is payable at the same time, ie by 31 March following the end of the year of assessment.

Investment incentives

In the free-trade zones, investors benefit from a guaranteed tax holiday and there are no import or export duties (except for sales made from free-trade zones into main UAE and the rest of the Gulf Cooperation Council (GCC) countries, namely Bahrain, Qatar, Kuwait, Oman and Saudi Arabia).

The length of the tax holiday varies between the free-trade zones – from 15 to 50 years. It is generally renewable at the discretion of the relevant free-trade zone authority.

Depreciation
Rates of depreciation for specific items are included in the income tax decrees. The straight-line depreciation method is commonly used in the UAE.

Allowable business expenses and deductions
Taxable income is defined as the net income arising through the conduct of a trade or business in the emirate after permitted deductions are made. Deductions are allowed for costs and expenses incurred regardless of where the expense was incurred. In practice, general provisions are disallowed until such time as the expense is incurred or a bad debt is written off. Specific provisions, provided they are reasonably calculated, are sometimes allowed.

The deduction of losses sustained in connection with carrying on trade or business, including bad debts, is allowed. Tax losses that were surplus in the previous year can be carried forward for relief in future years. However, some emirates impose a limit of two years on the carry-forward in the case of branches of foreign banks. There is no provision for carrying losses back.

The Abu Dhabi Tax Decree allows establishment expenses to be deducted but the Dubai Tax Decree restricts the deduction for pre-trading expenses to 10 per cent per annum. There is no provision in the tax decrees for appeals and it is difficult to have a decision reviewed once made. Due to the nature of the tax legislation the treatment of various items of income and expenditure can only be decided with certainty on entering into discussions with the tax authorities on a case-by-case basis.

Book-keeping and corporate assessments
The taxpayers accounting records can be maintained using either the accruals or cash receipts and disbursements method.

Other taxes and employer's contributions

Social security taxes
Employers of UAE nationals in the private sector are required to pay monthly contributions of 12.5 per cent of the employee's wage. Public-sector employers contribute 15 per cent. An additional contribution of 5 per cent is borne by the employee.

Capital gains
There is no specific capital gains tax legislation in the UAE. For entities subject to taxation, gains arising on the disposal of capital assets are taxed as part of taxable income.

Miscellaneous taxes

Value-added tax (VAT)
There is no VAT in the UAE.

Stamp duty and transfer taxes
Apart from a 2 per cent registration fee on the transfer of legal title in respect of property acquisitions, there is no other transfer tax in the UAE.

Municipality tax
Municipality taxes are charged in some of the emirates. In Dubai a 10 per cent tax is charged on hotel revenues (usually passed on to the consumer as a service charge). Rented premises are taxed at the rate of 10 per cent for commercial and 5 per cent for residential premises. Abu Dhabi does not levy a municipality tax on rented premises, but landlords are required to pay certain annual licence fees (which they may/may not indirectly pass to the tenant).

Customs duties
From 1 January 2003 the GCC states formed the GCC Customs Union, which imposes a unified tariff of 5 per cent on most goods entering the GCC. Certain goods are exempted from the duty, eg some foodstuffs, commodities and medicines. Most GCC states also have a list of items that are subject to a higher rate of duty. These items are usually those produced by the GCC state concerned and higher duty is imposed in an attempt to protect the national industry from imported goods. In some of the member states certain goods, eg those against the principles of Islam are prohibited for import.

Customs duty is charged at the first point of entry into the GCC and goods may then move freely between member states without payment of further duty. There is an interim 'phasing in' period of three years during which the formalities and paperwork requirements between each member country are being finalized. Goods entering free-trade zones are exempt from customs duty on entry, but customs duty is payable on exit if they are destined for one of the GCC member states – including main UAE.

4.5

Commercial Agencies in the UAE

Marwan Awad, Trowers & Hamlins, Dubai

Introduction

Although entities located outside of the UAE may sell directly to customers in the UAE without using an intermediary such as an agent, by law only UAE nationals or wholly UAE-owned entities may conduct certain 'commercial agency activities' within the UAE. While there is no precise definition of 'commercial agency', the practical effect of this restriction precludes foreigners located inside of the UAE from distributing imported products or services in the UAE. As such, foreign service providers and manufacturers of products who wish to penetrate the UAE market often find it necessary either to engage a UAE commercial agent or other UAE representative or to establish a licensed presence in the UAE – usually in the form of a limited liability company – to undertake the desired activity. Since establishment of a licensed presence requires a more significant investment of time and money, and may be subject to limitations with respect to the licensed activities, foreign parties often opt to appoint a UAE agent or representative to act on their behalf.

One should note that there are other relationships between foreign entities and UAE parties that do not constitute commercial agencies. For instance, foreign branch offices generally are required to engage a UAE national agent or 'service agent' and this relationship does not fall under the ambit of commercial agency regulations as described below. Local service agents perform administrative functions for the foreign party and should not be confused with commercial agents.

All foreign entities engaging an agent or other representative for the UAE should be aware of the application and impact of UAE law on such a relationship. This chapter focuses on the legal requirements and practical aspects of setting up commercial agency and distributorship agreements in the UAE, as well as addressing the termination of a commercial agency.

Commercial agency law

The UAE Commercial Agency Law (Federal Law No.18 of 1981, as amended by Federal Law No.14 of 1988) (the Commercial Agency Law) regulates and governs the appointment of commercial agents, sales representatives and distributors in the UAE. The ambit of the Commercial Agency Law is quite broad as it encompasses any arrangement in which a foreign company is represented by a local agent for the distribution, offer, sale or marketing of a product or service within the UAE against payment of a fixed commission or profit. This definition has been broadened somewhat by Article 197 of Federal Law No. 18 of 1993 (the Commercial Code), which simply states that 'an agency shall be commercial when it is concerned with commercial activities'. These definitions clearly cover agency and distribution, and were held by the Dubai Court of First Instance also to cover franchise. In practice, the Commercial Agency Law makes no distinction between commissioned agents, distributors who purchase for their own account, franchisees and sales representatives.

Requirements for the commercial agent

Pursuant to Article 2 of the Commercial Agency Law, only UAE nationals or companies wholly owned by UAE nationals may legally be appointed commercial agents. Article 4 requires that the relationship between the principal and agent be governed by a written and notarized agreement and, further, in accordance with Article 3, the agent should register that agreement in the Register of Commercial Agents maintained by the Federal Ministry of Economy and Planning (formerly known as the Ministry of Economy and Commerce).

Requirements for the commercial agency agreement

Authentication and notarization requirements

In order to be registered, the commercial agency agreement must be an executed written document that has been notarized. If both parties sign the agreement in the UAE, it can be prepared in Arabic only or in dual Arabic/English text. The representative of the foreign principal will usually furnish a fully authenticated and officially translated document regarding power of attorney and, in some cases, a board resolution that authorizes the issuance of the power of attorney.

If the foreign principal wishes to sign abroad, the agency agreement can be prepared in English (or other native language assuming it can be officially translated into Arabic), signed by the foreign principal, notarized, legalized and sent to the UAE for authentication before the UAE Ministry of Foreign Affairs, and then officially translated. A search may be carried out at the Register of Commercial Agents to determine whether, in fact, the commercial agency is registered within the UAE.

Appointment of agents and recognition by courts
The appointment of a commercial agent must be exclusive although it is possible to have a different agent for each of the seven emirates. One common approach is to appoint one agent for Abu Dhabi and another for Dubai and the northern emirates due in part to the fact that, in practice, commerce is often separated by such geographic distinction. Appointing a different agent for some or all of the emirates may also be a useful tool for damage limitation on termination but may not necessarily be sensible from a practical point of view.

The commercial agency agreement can cover the principal's entire range of products or services for a territory, or only a limited number of specific products or services offered by the foreign principal. The commercial agent must also supply the necessary and adequate spare parts, equipment, materials and accessories for maintenance of any durable goods they import.

Unless a commercial agency is registered, it will not be recognized as a proper agency and, consequently, will not have the protection provided by law; further, the courts should not hear any lawsuits filed by either the principal or agent. All registered agreements will be subject to UAE law even if the agreement states otherwise. Additionally, all such agreements will be subject to the jurisdiction of the UAE courts and, generally, any decisions regarding enforcement issued by a foreign court will not be enforceable in the UAE.

Although Article 3 of the Commercial Agency Law stipulates that only registered agents may be engaged in the business of commercial agencies, there are currently no official sanctions in not complying with this; as mentioned above, the main repercussion is that the parties will not be provided the protection afforded by UAE law. However, UAE courts have been known to recognize a claim brought by a UAE agent with regard to an unregistered commercial agency agreement.

Statutory rights of the commercial agent

Commercial agents are granted formidable statutory rights under the Commercial Agency Law that are designed to protect an agent who may expend considerable efforts, including monetary expenses, to build a profitable market for the products or services. Some of these statutory rights are outlined below.

- Commercial agents are entitled to receive commissions on sales of the specified products or services in their designated territory irrespective of whether such sales are made by or through the agent.
- Since all registered commercial agency agreements are treated as exclusive (even if the agreement is silent on this, or indicates that the agency is non-exclusive), registered agents are entitled to prevent products subject to their agency from being imported into their designated territory if the agent is not the consignee.
- No registration of a new commercial agent in the territory of an existing commercial agent for the same products or services will be allowed until the existing arrangement is terminated (i) with the agreement of the existing agent or (ii) with substantial justification as determined by the Commercial Agency Committee (with an appeal procedure to the UAE courts being available).

Due to these protections, foreign companies must consider very carefully the person or entity they choose as their commercial agent. While the protections are designed to protect hardworking local agents, they also benefit those who choose not to perform as expected and can work to prevent a foreign principal from replacing an underperforming agent unless the foreign principal pays compensation to the agent.

Termination of a registered agency agreement

Once a foreign principal enters into an agency agreement that is registered, it can be extremely difficult to terminate without the agent filing a claim for compensation, which is usually based upon the agent's future loss of profit. Without proof of substantial justification by the foreign principal, commercial agents are normally entitled to receive compensation from the principal if (i) the agency agreement is terminated or (ii) if the agency agreement is not renewed.

However, it can be extremely difficult to show reasons that the Commercial Agency Committee or UAE courts regard as sufficiently substantial. At the least there must be a clear breach of contract fundamental to the relationship of principal and agent, which will usually revolve around the lack of activity or unsuccessful activity of the agent. In the event of termination the onus is on the agent to prove that he/she would be caused loss or would be deprived of the benefit expected from his/her efforts due to the termination or non-renewal of the agreement.

With regard to the assessment of damages, as a rule of thumb, at least three years' loss of profits is usually awarded to an aggrieved agent and in calculating such damages, the onus would again be on the agent to prove such losses. As litigation in the UAE is both costly and protracted for both parties and could take several years before a conclusion is reached with the added factor that, regardless of the outcome, costs awarded by the UAE courts are minimal and rarely compensate the parties for the legal fees and time incurred, it is always advisable to enter into settlement negotiations when seeking to terminate a registered agency agreement.

Enforcement of the commercial agency agreement

The Commercial Agency Law establishes a Commercial Agency Committee that considers disputes regarding registered commercial agency agreements. The committee is authorized to appoint experts as it deems necessary to assist in the review of disputes. However, decisions of the Commercial Agency Committee do not necessarily constitute final judgements and either party may file an action with the UAE courts where the matter may be subject to *de novo* review under the normal judicial process of each emirate.

General observations regarding commercial agents

The statutory protections of commercial agents under the Commercial Agency Law create an obvious disincentive to foreign entities to do business through registered commercial agency agreements if alternative means are available. Due to the abovementioned difficulties concerning compensation on termination, some foreign principals prefer to operate on the basis of unregistered. As regards private-sector sales, foreign principals may be able to locate a UAE party willing to act as sales representative or distributor other than pursuant to a registered commercial agency agreement, assuming the party's trade licence authorizes it to undertake such activities. However, should any future action need to be taken against the agent by the principal, unless the commercial agency is registered, it will not be recognized as a proper agency and consequently will not have the protection provided by law and, further, the courts will not hear any lawsuits filed with regard to an unregistered agency.

Although this type of arrangement is possible, it is likely to make it more difficult for the foreign party to make public-sector sales. In addition, many commercial agents will insist on a registered agreement in order to avail themselves of the protection of the Commercial Agency

Law. The foreign principal may be forced into this position if it desires to appoint a UAE party with significant influence within the territory.

If the decision is made to pursue business through a registered commercial agency agreement, the foreign principal must undertake a thorough due diligence investigation of the proposed agent in order to ensure the long-term relationship will be formed with a reputable agent. An agreement should be carefully drafted that takes full advantage of the protections available to a foreign principal entering into such an arrangement.

In recent years there has been much discussion regarding modification of the Commercial Agency Law to be less protective of the local UAE agents or distributors. This stems, in part, from the general liberalization of the UAE economy, and as part of the UAE's efforts and desire to satisfy further the requirements of the World Trade Organization (WTO), of which it became a member on 10 April 1996. Although at the time of its entry to the WTO, the UAE secured certain exemptions and limitations from its obligations, these expired as of 2005.

The foregoing overview of commercial agencies in the UAE is not intended as a substitute for legal advice on specific matters. The writer does not accept any liability from the use or reliance on the information contained herein. The information stated above is current to March 2005.

4.6

Commercial Legislation for Doing Business in Dubai

Data Management and Business Research Department, DCCI

Requirements of practising business activity in economic sectors in Dubai and investment procedure

Practising any business activity, whether commercial or professional, should be through a body corporate, which requires choosing one of the legal forms for the firm that shall practise such activity. Subsequently, it is a substantial requirement for the competent authorities in charge of issuing licences to practise various activities, hence get engaged in the required business and start legal transactions relating thereto.

Therefore, choosing the right legal form for the firm should be subject to many considerations to be carefully studied so that the firm may conduct its business in the way for which it has been established, and also to be able to maintain the continuity that it derives from the stability of its legal status. The following considerations are some of those that should be observed in choosing the legal form of the firm.

- Compliance with the laws and legislation regulating the civil and commercial dealings and observing their provisions and rules is imperative as there are certain types of commercial companies that are not allowed to practise certain types of activities. For instance, limited liability companies are not allowed to practise the activity of insurance and exchange. Also, there are certain activities that are not allowed to be practised except by certain legal forms; for example, firms specialized in legal consultancy and accounting services cannot practise their activities except through professional companies.

- The size of the invested capital to be employed for practising the activity depends either on the personal ability of the investor in providing the required capital or his/her ability to raise funds from different financing sources in a lawful manner. Thus projects that need investment of huge funds for their implementation may require establishment of a public shareholding company in order to ensure securing the required capital.
- It is important to note the scope of the firm's activities and whether it is planning to practise its activities on the local, regional or international levels.
- The nationality of the investor needs to be noted. Local investors may practise most types of business activities through a sole proprietorship or any other form of company by entering into partnership with others but if the investor is not a local, then he/she needs, in most cases, to have a local partner in order to be able to practise certain business activities, except for the special cases where the law does not dictate such requirement.

In addition to other considerations, the investor has absolute discretion in choosing the legal form for practising his/her business except for the few cases for which the law has determined that they be practised through a certain legal form.

Establishing national firms and companies

Establishing sole proprietorship

The law permits the establishment of a sole proprietorship for UAE nationals, nationals of the Gulf Cooperation Council (GCC) countries and for other non-nationals (for certain types of business activities). Since the procedure and conditions differ in every case, the following is a list of conditions applied to each case for establishing sole proprietorship.

When the investor is a national individual

In this case, the national individual who wishes to practise a business activity may apply to the Department of Economic Development (DED) on the form specified for such purposes and in accordance with the licensing procedures.

When the investor is a citizen of one of the GCC states
In accordance with Article (8) of the Unified Economic Agreement in respect of treating all nationals of the GCC countries as nationals of any member state without any discrimination in carrying out business activities in the fields of industry, agriculture, livestock, fisheries and contracting, the beneficiary of such a licence in the UAE must be the actual conductor and, further, totally devoted to practise the profession for which he/she is licensed and in compliance with the provisions of Article (10) of the executive regulations and the Federal Law No. (2) of 1979.

Pursuant to the Federal Law No. 2 of 1989, concerning permitting citizens of GCC countries to conduct retail and wholesale trade in the country, of which the first article stated that it is permitted to the nationals of the GCC states, whether they are natural or juridical persons, to practice retail and wholesale trade in the UAE according to the rules and controls stipulated by a cabinet resolution.

Incorporation of commercial companies
According to Federal Law No 8 for 1984, as amended by Law No 13 for 1988, a commercial company shall be either 100 per cent owned by nationals or one in which nationals own at least 51 per cent of the capital. Article 5 of the law stipulates that commercial companies incorporated in the UAE shall take one of the following legal forms.

Joint liability company
A joint liability company comprises two or more partners whose liability for the company's debts extends to all their personal assets. That is why the law makes such a company exclusive to UAE nationals as foreigners tend to keep their money abroad, which renders the application of this condition impractical. The following conditions should be taken into consideration in incorporating a joint liability company:

- Company's name shall include names of all partners. It may, however, be confined to one or more names of partners and may carry an indication to the existence of the company. Such a company may also have a trade name of its own. If a non-partner's name is mentioned with his/her knowledge, he/she shall be held jointly responsible for the company's liabilities. Each partner shall be considered as trader and if the company goes bankrupt so shall all partners.

- Company's shares shall not take the form of negotiable deeds. All partners shall be jointly responsible for the company's liabilities with such responsibility extending to all their personal assets; any agreement to the contrary shall not be valid vis-à-vis third parties.

Limited partnership (partnership in commendam)

A limited partnership consists of one or more joint partners (whose liability for the company's debts extends to all their personal assets) and of one or more limited partners, whose liability to the company is limited to the value of their respective shares in the capital. All partners must be UAE nationals by law. The company's name shall include name(s) of one or more joint partners and indication to the existence of a company.

The company may also have a trade name of its own. A limited partner should not be referred to in the company's name. However, if his/her name is included with his/her knowledge, he/she shall be considered by *mala fide* third parties as a joint partner.

As far as joint partners are concerned, a limited partnership company shall be deemed as a joint liability company with rules of the latter applicable to it, provided however that the following stipulations be observed:

1. In addition to other data, limited partnership articles of association shall also include each limited partner's name, surname, nationality, date of birth, domicile, capital share and the paid-up portion.
2. A limited partner's liability to the company's creditors is limited to his/her share in the capital.
3. A limited partner shall not intervene in management affairs related to third parties even if he/she is empowered to do so. He/she may take part in the internal administration within the limits stated in the partnership agreement. He/she may seek to acquire copy of the profit and loss statement and balance sheet and verify their authenticity by viewing company records and documents, either by him/herself or through an agent from among the partners or others, provided that such an act does not cause any damage to the company.
4. If a limited partner violates the above conditions, he/she shall be held responsible, with all his/her assets, for liabilities arising as a result of his/her acts.
5. A limited partner may be held accountable, with all his/her money, for all liabilities of the company if he/she acted in a way that caused a third party to believe that he/she is absolutely one of the joint partners. In such a case, he/she shall be subject to the rules applicable to joint partners.
6. If a limited partner carried out banned administrative acts by virtue of an explicit or implicit authority from the acting partners,

these partners shall be held jointly responsible for the liabilities arising from such acts.

7. Resolutions of a limited partnership company are adopted by unanimous vote of joint and limited partners, unless it is stated in the contract that a majority vote shall suffice.
8. Resolutions on amending the company's articles of association shall be valid only if taken by a unanimous vote of joint and limited partners.

Limited liability company

A limited liability company is one incorporated by at least two but not more than 50 partners, and whose objectives do not include insurance, banking and capital investment for third parties. The company's capital shall not be less than AED300,000 divided into equal shares of no less than AED1,000 each. These shares shall not be in the form of negotiable deeds. In the event that a local body corporate becomes a founding partner in the new company, the new company's capital shall not be less than two-fold of the capital of that body corporate.

Where non-nationals are participating in a limited liability company, the share of nationals shall not be less than 51 per cent of the company's capital (economic activities exclusively reserved for nationals should be taken into account). A limited liability company shall have a name derived from its objectives or from names of one or more partners. The name shall also show the words 'limited liability company' and the capital amount. A limited liability company may carry out any permissible activity, except insurance, banking and capital investment for third parties. It shall not resort to public subscription for setting up or increasing its capital or for acquiring loans. Moreover, the company is not allowed to issue negotiable shares or stocks.

Capital shares of the company are indivisible, and if they are owned by many individuals those shall select one of them to act as sole proprietor and represent them vis-à-vis the company. The company may fix a deadline for that selection and shall have the right, after the lapse of that deadline, to sell out the shares on behalf of the holders. In such a case, the partners shall have pre-emptive rights to such shares. Profits and losses shall be equally apportioned among the shareholders unless otherwise stated in the articles of association. A partner's share shall be transferred to his/her heirs and devisees (who shall enjoy the same rights as the heirs).

A limited liability company shall be run by one or more managers (not to exceed five), to be selected from among the partners or others. The managers shall be appointed, either in the articles of association or a separate contract, for a fixed or unfixed term. In the event that the managers are not appointed in the same manner as defined in the previous paragraph, they shall be appointed by the general assembly of partners. Unless his/her powers are defined in the articles of association, the manager shall have full power to run the company and take actions binding upon the company provided he/she explains the capacity upon which he/she took such actions. A manager's responsibility is comparable to that of the directors and anything to the contrary in the articles of association shall be null and void.

Public joint stock company

A public joint stock company is one whose capital is divided into equal, negotiable stocks, and where a partner is accountable only to the extent of his/her share in the company. The capital must be sufficient for realizing the company's objectives, but it shall in no case be less than AED10 million. As the company issues negotiable shares, it should be subject to the pertinent control measures. Founders of a public joint stock company are obliged by law to issue the articles of incorporation and articles of association.

No such company shall be licensed unless it has at least 10 founders. Upon approval of the incorporation application by the DED, shares are offered for subscription. Subscribers are then invited to a general assembly to elect a board of directors and declare the company established. Founders shall then submit a request to the Minister of Economy and Commerce to declare the company incorporated.

The company shall have a name derived from its objectives; it should not be that of a natural person except where the purpose of the company is to invest in a patent registered under the name of that person, or where it has acquired, upon or after incorporation, a store and assumed its name. In all cases, the term 'joint stock company' shall be added to the company's name. A joint stock company shall not carry a name identical with or similar to another company's. Should this happen, the other company may ask the concerned administrative or judicial authorities to force that company to change its name.

A founder is anyone who signs the initial partnership contract and articles of association of the company with the intention of bearing the responsibility rising thereof. No joint stock company will be licensed unless it has at least 10 founders. Notwithstanding the foregoing, the federal government or any of the governments of the Federation's member emirates may set up a company, either solely or in association with a fewer number of partners than that provided for in the preceding paragraph.

Founders may select from, among themselves, a committee of no less than three and not more than five members to follow up the incorporation formalities with the concerned authorities. Founders shall subscribe to not less than 20 per cent but not to exceed 40 per cent of the company's capital and pay, before the subscription statement is published, the amount equivalent to the amount due from the subscribers for each share upon subscription. Before inviting public subscription, the founders shall furnish the Ministry of Economy and Commerce and the concerned authorities with a certificate by the bank to which the amount is deposited, to verify that the foregoing percentage has been paid.

The company's capital is made up of equal shares with a nominal value of not less than AED1 but not more AED100. Upon incorporation, no shares shall be issued at less than their nominal value plus issuance expenses. All the company's shares shall have equal rights and liabilities. Shares shall be nominal and negotiable. No share-to-bearer shall be issued. However, profit bonds, the form and rules of which shall be determined by the company's articles of association, may either be nominal or issued to bearer.

Private joint stock company

A private joint stock company is one founded by at least three persons and does not offer its shares for public subscription. Rather, founders subscribe to the entire capital, which shall not be less than AED2 million. Other than that, it shall be subject to the same provisions applicable to public joint stock companies. Such a company shall be set up in accordance with the terms and conditions as laid down for public joint stock companies, save for the provisions on public subscription. A private joint stock company may convert into a public joint stock company if:

- the nominal value of its issued shares has been paid in full;
- it has been in existence for at least two consecutive years;
- it has realized, during the two years preceding the conversion application, net profits allocable to shareholders equivalent in average to at least 10 per cent of the capital; and
- a resolution on conversion is adopted by an extraordinary general meeting and passed by a majority of partners representing three-quarters of the capital.

Share partnership

This is a company made up of joint partners (whose liability for the company's debts extends to all their personal assets) and limited partners (whose liability is limited to the value of their respective shares in the capital). Such a company is considered a joint liability company as far as the joint partners are concerned. A joint partner is regarded as a trader even if he/she has not had such a capacity before joining the company. All joint partners must be UAE nationals. The company's capital shall be divided into negotiable shares of equal value. The company's name shall be derived from the name(s) of one or more joint partners. A unique name or one derived from its objective may be added.

Share partnership companies are subject to all incorporation rules applicable to public joint stock companies, save for the following:

- All joint partners and other founders shall sign the company's articles of association and articles of incorporation. They shall be treated similarly, in terms of responsibility, to the founders of joint stock companies.
- The company's articles of association and articles of incorporation shall show the joint partners' names, surnames, nationalities and domiciles.
- The company's capital shall not be less than AED500,000.
- Deeds issued by share partnerships shall be subject to the same rules applicable to joint stock companies.

A share partnership shall be set up in accordance with the terms and conditions applicable to joint stock companies, except for the rules on public subscription.

Particular partnership

This is a company made up of two or more partners to share profits and losses from one or more business activities carried out by one of them in his/her own name. Such a company is restricted to the relationship between the partners and does not apply to others. This type of company shall neither be entered in the commercial register nor declared. Particular partnerships are not allowed to issue negotiable shares or bonds. A shareholder in such a company is not considered a trader unless he/she carries out business transactions by him/herself. Third parties may only have recourse to the partner with whom they deal. Should partners reveal anything that suggests to third parties that a company exists, such a company may be considered as an existing company whose partners are jointly liable toward third parties.

A particular partnership is in fact a 'concealed' company. It invests in a particular enterprise in the name of one of its partners. For instance, a holder of a commercial licence may opt to have others share the burden of running the company with him/her. No special licence shall be issued for the company. It will suffice to use the licence issued to the original partner who may wish to take others as partners in setting up an enterprise, investing the licence or running the company's activities. Although not subject to registration and declaration, such a partnership is deemed valid and binding and can be attested at the notary public.

Incorporation of professional (civil) companies

A professional company refers to a contract by two or more persons to carry out work for third parties for consideration, depending mainly on their mental effort, whether they be equal or unequal in work distribution provided that the works are unified or carried out simultaneously.* Hence, professional companies are those formed by professionals and craftsmen for conducting non-trade activities. The Trading Transactions Act, promulgated by Federal Law No. 18 for 1993, stipulates explicitly under Article 15 that the merchant status does not apply to the government ministries, departments, authorities, public corporations, public utilities, associations, clubs or freelance professionals who do not practise trading activities. However, the business activities practised by these parties shall be subject to the Act unless specifically exempted.

Also, according to Clause 4 of the Local Order No. 63 for 1991, regarding licensing professionals and craftsmen in the emirate of Dubai, natural persons may associate to practise professional or craft work by themselves, by setting up a business company pursuant to Articles 683 to 690 of the Federal Civil Transactions Law. If all the licencees are non-nationals, they must have a 'local services agent' whose liability toward his/her principals and third parties shall be limited to provision of the reasonable experience that enables him/her to conduct professional work, without assuming any civil or financial liability in connection with his/her principals' business activities, within or outside the emirate. However, the relation between the two parties shall be governed by a service agency contract.

Activities undertaken by professional companies

Professional companies shall conduct specific activities, such as legal advocacy and consultancy, auditing and keeping of accounting books, civil and architectural engineering consultancy and services, administrative and economic consultancy and studies, technical services, health and medical treatment services, educational services etc.

Rules governing professional companies

- Each partner shall undertake to perform the work undertaken by him/her, and shall have the right to receive the agreed charge. A partner does not have to carry out the work by him/herself; rather,

* This text has been taken from Federal Law No. 5 of 1985 on the issuance of the UAE's Civil Transaction Law.

he/she may assign it to another partner or any other person, unless the client requires him/her to do it by him/herself.

- Profit shall be distributed among the partners as mutually agreed. Their respective shares in the profit may vary, even if they have an equal share of duties. Each partner shall receive his/her profit share even if he/she could not do his/her share of the work, due to a valid excuse. Professional companies may be established on the understanding that some partners provide the premises, machinery and equipment while others do the work.
- Partners remain jointly liable for proper discharge of the work.

Licensing procedures

Licensing procedures for professional companies follow the following order:

- preparing the partnership contract according to the established rules;
- attesting the contract according to the law;
- filing a licence application, in the appropriate form, to the DED according to the procedures set forth.

Establishing foreign sole proprietorship, partnership in national companies and establishing branches of foreign companies and representative offices

Establishing foreign sole proprietorship

The foreign investor is permitted to practise certain types of business activities allowed for non-nationals without having a national partner, eg to practise some specialized professions such as providing medical services, engineering consultancies, legal practice and consultancies, computer consultancies and similar services, provided that such an investor holds a valid and legal UAE residence permit. Also, it is a condition that he/she should have a local services agent according to a service agency contract authenticated by the notary public. Afterwards, the residence of such an investor should be under the sponsorship of the same business under which he/she practises his/her activity.

After complying with the required terms and conditions, the investor may apply to the DED on the form specified for such purposes for obtaining the licence to practise the required activity, attached with the required documents in accordance with the procedures for licensing.

Appointment of a commercial agent

A foreign company can market its products within the UAE by appointment of a commercial agent subject to the provisions of the Commercial Agencies Law No. 18 of 1981. A commercial agent as per this law is not the legal agent as defined in the Civil Transactions Code and Commercial Transactions Law. In these two laws the agent may bind the principals in the matters for which he/she is authorized and he/she may conduct commercial transaction in his/her name and deal with others on behalf of the principal. In the Commercial Agencies Law, however, the commercial agent is a merchant conducting his/her activities independently of the principal and deals with others in his/her name and cannot in any way bind the principal in such dealings or transactions. He/she merely purchases products or services from the principal as per an independent sale agreement and then sells the same to his/her clients as per other agreements.

Obligations of the principal towards the agent are confined to what is stipulated in the agency agreement. The definition of the agent in the Commercial Agencies Law is the same as that of the exclusive distributor in foreign laws. Perhaps this is what motivated some agents to call this agency a distribution agency and name the agent as distributor. It is preferable to use an exclusive distributor and there is no objection to naming an agent as such as per the provisions of the law or in the light of practices of the Ministry of Economy and Commerce. As per the provisions of the law an agent is defined as the person who handles the products or services of the principal by exclusive sale or distribution within the territory of the agency.

As per the practices of the Ministry of Economy and Commerce, a commercial agency agreement is registered no matter what it is called, as long as it complies with the basic elements required by the law. Most important of these elements is that dealing should be exclusively with one agent, attestation as required by the law, that the agreement should not contain provisions violating what is stipulated in the law and it should be stated that it is an agency agreement as per the provisions of the Commercial Agencies Law or the agent is appointed as per the provisions of the above law. Therefore the agency agreement should include the following:

- The agent should be an exclusive agent. In other words he/she should monopolize distribution of the products or services of the principal in the agency territory, which should be either all of the UAE or any part thereof, such as one or some of the seven emirates.

- The agent should be a UAE national if a natural person. If the agent is a body corporate (eg company), it is conditional that all the partners be UAE nationals.
- The agency agreement should be registered with the Ministry of Economy and Commerce. This registration will provide the agent with enough protection, as it will prohibit the entry of any products or services that are the subject matter of the agency agreement to the UAE through any other party other than the agent or those licensed to do so by the agent. The agency agreement cannot be terminated even if it was for a limited period except through the two methods as stipulated by the law. The agency is not allowed to register a new agency agreement for any other agent concerning products or services that are the subject matter of a registered agency agreement unless the previous agency is cancelled from the Commercial Agencies Register at the Ministry of Economy and Commerce.
- If a dispute arises between the principal and the agent, the principal may terminate the agency agreement by one of two methods: either by cordial agreement with the agent or to refer the matter to the commercial agencies committee at the Ministry of Economy and Commerce. The committee will assess the reasons for which the principal wishes to terminate the agency agreement and will settle the dispute accordingly. The purpose in assigning the authority of terminating the agency agreement to the Ministry of Economy and Commerce is not intended to make termination impossible but to make the decision for termination be based on objective reasons as assessed by a non-biased authority enlightened in commercial affairs and problems. Therefore a decision is not left to personal judgement and will not be based on a subjective or arbitrary discretion of one party.

Establishing branches of companies and representative offices

The Companies Law, in Article (313), allows a foreign company to exercise its main activity in the UAE or open an office, branch or representative office. The foreign company that opens a branch in the UAE may exercise freely the activities for which it is licensed. Of course such licence is governed by certain provisions of the law and executive regulations. Legally there are certain activities confined to UAE nationals – such as banking, money investment, insurance – and commercial agencies. The executive regulations include the conditions and procedure for licensing followed by the DED, which are issued from time to time in the form of by-laws or local orders.

The company that opens a representative office in the UAE may practise promotional business for the products and services provided by the parent company and facilitate contacts between the company and its UAE clients. However, the office is not licensed to conduct business operations or marketing directly in whatever manner such as obtaining credit facilities, submitting offers etc.

The main stipulation for opening an office or a branch of a foreign company in the UAE is to appoint a service agent, who should be a UAE national. The law provides that such an agent is not an empowered agent who can bind his/her principal, as explained in the definition of the term 'agent' in the Commercial Companies Law. In actual fact, he/she is not an agent in any sense. Article (314) of the companies law defines the legal status of such agent. It provides that such an agent is not responsible to undertake any financial obligations concerning the activities of the company's branch or office within the UAE or abroad. He/she should not interfere in the matters related to the company's management or activities. His/her duties towards the company and others are confined to providing such services as required by the principal. These services usually include the obtaining of entry or residence visas, the acquiring of the necessary licences or facilitating the processing of its transactions with the government authorities, eg submitting tenders, following them up and notifying the foreign company of all the announcements related thereto, and following up the company's needs and affairs and keeping it informed of the same.

The service agent is remunerated in a lump sum for the services rendered to the foreign company, with the sum being the subject of an agreement between him/her and the company. Furthermore, the service agent should be a UAE national or, if a body corporate (company), that body should be wholly owned by nationals.

Procedure for establishing branches of foreign companies and representative offices

With the exception of those companies licensed to practise activities in the UAE free zones, foreign companies are not allowed to practise activities in Dubai or to establish offices or branches unless they obtain a licence issued by the Ministry of Economy and Commerce after the approval of DED. The licence issued shall determine the activity the company is allowed to practise.

Foreign companies licensed to operate in the UAE may not start their activities before being inscribed in the ministry's Register of

Foreign Companies, the Commercial Register at DED and obtaining the Department's Trade Licence. To set up a branch of a foreign company the following steps should be observed:

- An application shall be submitted to the Department of Companies at the Office of the Ministry of Economy and Commerce in Dubai. The application should include the following data:
  - name, type of the company and address of its main office;
  - type of activity, specialization or type of operations required to be practised in the UAE;
  - main operations carried out by the company abroad and its previous expertise in the field of the activity in which it intends to conduct business; and
  - name of the local services agent in the UAE and his/her address if he/she is a natural person; if the service agent is a corporate body (company) its legal form, capital, names of the shareholders and their addresses should be included. All of the shareholders should be UAE nationals.
- The Department of Companies at the Ministry of Economy and Commerce, after registering the application giving it a number and making sure that the required documents are complete, shall refer it to DED as follows:
  - In case of rejection, the application and the attached documents shall be returned to the Department of Companies to be kept there and the concerned parties shall be notified of the rejection decision.
  - In case of acceptance, the application shall be referred to the Committee of Foreign Companies at the ministry for approving the content of the application and for determining the activity of the branch. This committee shall prepare its recommendations and refer them to the Minister of Economy and Commerce for issuing his/her decision. The Department of Companies at the Ministry shall then issue the licensing decision.
- Completion of registration procedure in the Commercial Register and issuance of the trade licence by the licensing department at DED.
- Registration of the company's branch with the Dubai Chamber of Commerce and Industry.

- Inscription of the company's branch in the Foreign Companies' Register at the Ministry of Economy and Commerce.

The Executive Regulation of the Law set general requirements with which the foreign companies should comply. They include the following:

- Each foreign company granted a licence to operate in the UAE should have an auditor, provided that he/she is licensed and his/her name is inscribed in the Chartered Accountants' Register.
- Any company practising activities in the UAE and wishing to amend the data according to which it obtained the licence, should approach the Department of Commercial Affairs at the Ministry of Economy and Commerce through its concerned office to notify it of such amendments.
- Foreign companies licensed to practise activities in the UAE, should renew their inscription in the Register of Foreign Companies annually and one month prior to the expiry date of registration.
- In case the company wishes to cease its activity, it should apply to the ministry requesting the cancellation of its inscription in the Foreign Companies Register and the business of the company shall not be deemed to have ceased unless the ministry's decree is issued, approving the cancellation.
- All documents pertaining to foreign companies shall be submitted to the Ministry of Economy and Commerce in Arabic, and if they were written in a foreign language, a duly certified Arabic translation should be attached thereto.

Partnership in national companies

UAE nationals are confined to only one type of commercial company, which is the partnership company. Partnership in commendam and partnership limited by shares, as stipulated by the laws, are open to foreign participation. However, partnership limited by shares does not suit non-national investors as it is stipulated that management shall be undertaken by the joint partner and profits must be divided as per capital participation. Therefore, the following legal forms are the most suitable for the foreign investors.

Limited liability company

A limited liability company is the most important type of company for non-nationals. It is stipulated that the number of partners should not be less than two and not more than 50. The law also provides that the share capital of this company should not be less than AED150,000. However, the competent authorities in Dubai made the minimum share capital AED300,000. The shares of such companies are not open for subscription by the public and are not negotiable. Non-national partners are permitted to hold shares not exceeding 49 per cent of the capital, however, profits may be divided on other ratios agreed upon, taking into consideration efforts of non-national partners in management, introduction of technology or providing expertise. Management of the company may be undertaken by the expatriate partner.

Joint stock company

The joint stock company in the UAE is as its corresponding type of company in other countries. The foreign partner may own up to 49 per cent of the shares for public subscription except in the companies whose activities are reserved for UAE nationals only. The capital of the public shareholding company should not be less than AED10 million. As it issues shares that are out to public subscription and traded in exchange markets, it is the subject to control procedure necessitated by such a status.

It may be useful to remark here that although, the law provides that the majority of the board directors and the president should be nationals, a later amendment permitted the choice of the vice-president to come from non-UAE shareholders. This clearly shows that the non-UAE shareholders can practise in the management of the company at the highest echelon, or it can be said in fact that the law accommodates a kind of marriage between the majority of capitals in giving it the office of president, and the need for practical experience in giving non-UAE members the office of vice-president.

The private shareholding company

Like the public shareholding company, this company issues shares, but not through public subscription. Capital should not be less than AED2 million and numbers of shareholders shall not be less than three. In other aspects this type of company is governed by the same provisions that are applicable to the public shareholding companies.

The joint venture company

The joint venture company is a clandestine company, the existence of which is known only to its partners and those contracting with it. It is principally suited for implementing a particular project licensed in the name of a local partner who whishes to join with another partner – who may be non-national – to set up such a company where the other partner can contribute not only capital but also knowhow and management.

Such a company need not be licensed as the licence of the local partner is sufficient to conduct the business of the company thereunder. Also it shall not be registered or published in the ministry's bulletin. Nevertheless, it is a sound firm contract legally binding on the partners and can be authenticated before the notary public. Although the capital of this company should be 51 per cent for the local partner and 49 per cent for the foreigner, the ratio of sharing the profits need not follow the capital sharing ratio, and the percentage of profit distribution may be otherwise, particularly if the foreign partner undertakes the management of the company in addition to contributing his/her share in the capital.

This type of company is deemed to provide an appropriate legal form for the relationship between the national and non-national partners better than 'the sleeping partner' resulting in side agreement practices. This shall put an end to these practices and problems resulting from them, which UAE courts have witnessed in recent years.

Procedures for establishing a company by entering into partnership with a UAE national

After choosing a national partner, whether he/she is a natural or juridical person, procedures for establishing the company and obtaining the licence can be processed as follows:

- procedures for establishing a company according to the Incorporation of Commercial Companies;
- procedures for obtaining trade licence from the business registration division in DED according to the licensing procedures; or
- procedures for the registration of the company with the Dubai Chamber of Commerce and Industry according to the Vision, Mission and Objectives of the Chamber.

Establishing foreign professional (civil) companies

Some companies that are practising non-commercial activities, such as professional firms set up by artisans, are usually not required to have a national partner. Based on this, the administrative Order No. (63) of 1991 was issued. This order allows non-national professionals to set up such companies subject to specific terms and conditions, most important of which is that the company should have a national service agent.

Investment of foreign capital in the free zones

A national partner is not required for foreign companies and non-nationals wanting to invest in the economic projects in the free zones; 100 per cent foreign ownership is possible. The establishment and licensing of such projects are subject to the procedures of the free zones.

Appendix

Appendix

Contributors' Contact Details

Abu Dhabi Chamber of Commerce and Industry (ADCCI)
PO Box 662
Abu Dhabi
UAE
Tel: +9712 617 7419
Fax: +9712 634 8954
Website: www.adcci.gov.ae

AXA Insurance (Gulf)
PO Box 290,
Dubai
UAE
Tel: +9714 324 3434
Fax: +9714 315 0215
Website: www.axa-gulf.com
Contact: Paul Holmes (Country Manager)

Dubai Chamber of Commerce and Industry (DCCI)
PO Box 1457
Dubai
UAE
Tel: +9714 228 0000
Fax: +9714 221 1646
Website: www.dcci.ae

Dubai International Financial Centre (DIFC)
Level 14
The Gate
PO Box 74777
Dubai
UAE
Tel: +9714 362 2445
Fax: +9714 362 2333
Website: www.difc.ae

Contact: Susan Ehtesham, Senior Brand Manager
Email: Susan.Ehtesham@difc.ae, Emad.Abourahme@difc.ae, Dana.Kablawi@difc.ae

InCite Research & Marketing Solutions
Tel: +9714 391 1991
Fax: + 9714 390 4644
Website: www.incite-research.com
Contact: Jan Stuffers, Managing Consultant
Email: jan.stuffers@incitemar.com, info@incite-research.com

KPMG Dubai
Tel: + 9714 403 0455
Mobile: + 9715 559 6514
Fax: +971 4 4030 47

Mellon Global Investments
PO Box 31303
Dubai
UAE
Tel: +9714 319 7624
Fax: +9714 319 7524
Website: www.mellonglobalinvestments.com
Contact: Nigel Sillitoe
Email: mgi-information@mellon.com

National Bank of Dubai (NBD)
Head Office
PO Box 777
Deira
Dubai
UAE
Tel: +9714 201 2204
Fax: +9714 221 0319
Contact: Rehana Aboul-Hosen, Media Coordinator

Trowers & Hamlins
Abu Dhabi
Butti Al Otaiba Building
Khalifa Street
PO Box 45628
Abu Dhabi
UAE
Tel: +9712 626 7274
Fax: +9712 626 7276

Contact: Nick White, Partner
Email: nwhite@trowers.com

Dubai
7th Floor
Rais Hassan Saadi Building
Mankhool Road
PO Box 23092
Dubai
UAE
Tel: +9714 351 9201
Fax: + 9714 351 9205
Contact: Edward Rose
Email: erose@trowers.com

Index

References in italic indicate figures or tables.